LEAD

EXPONENTIALLY

YOUR PATH TO DEVELOPING
AUTHENTIC AND INTENTIONAL LEADERS

LEAD
EXPONENTIALLY

REED NYFFELER

GREENLEAF
BOOK GROUP PRESS

This publication is designed to provide accurate and authoritative information in regard to the subject matter covered. It is sold with the understanding that the publisher and author are not engaged in rendering legal, accounting, or other professional services. Nothing herein shall create an attorney-client relationship, and nothing herein shall constitute legal advice or a solicitation to offer legal advice. If legal advice or other expert assistance is required, the services of a competent professional should be sought.

Published by Greenleaf Book Group Press
Austin, Texas
www.gbgpress.com

Copyright © 2025 Reed Nyffeler

All rights reserved.

Thank you for purchasing an authorized edition of this book and for complying with copyright law. No part of this book may be reproduced, stored in a retrieval system, or transmitted by any means, electronic, mechanical, photocopying, recording, or otherwise, without written permission from the copyright holder.

Distributed by Greenleaf Book Group

For ordering information or special discounts for bulk purchases, please contact Greenleaf Book Group at PO Box 91869, Austin, TX 78709, 512.891.6100.

Design and composition by Greenleaf Book Group
Cover design by Greenleaf Book Group

Scripture quotations are taken from the *Holy Bible*, New Living Translation, copyright ©1996, 2004, 2015 by Tyndale House Foundation. Used by permission of Tyndale House Publishers, Carol Stream, Illinois 60188. All rights reserved.

Publisher's Cataloging-in-Publication data is available.

Print ISBN: 979-8-88645-328-7

eBook ISBN: 979-8-88645-329-4

To offset the number of trees consumed in the printing of our books, Greenleaf donates a portion of the proceeds from each printing to the Arbor Day Foundation. Greenleaf Book Group has replaced over 50,000 trees since 2007.

Printed in the United States of America on acid-free paper

25 26 27 28 29 30 31 32   10 9 8 7 6 5 4 3 2 1

First Edition

CONTENTS

Preface vii

SECTION ONE: Why Develop Leaders?

Chapter 1: Potential   3

Chapter 2: Experiential   7

Chapter 3: Exponential   13

Chapter 4: Beneficial   19

SECTION TWO: Who Should You Develop?

Chapter 5: Character   29

Chapter 6: Charisma   37

Chapter 7: Committed   43

Chapter 8: Collaborative   49

Chapter 9: Connected   53

SECTION THREE: What Capacities Do Leaders Need?

Chapter 10: Visioning   61

Chapter 11: Strategic Planning   67

Chapter 12: Financial Acumen   73

Chapter 13: Team Development   83

Chapter 14: Project Management   93

SECTION FOUR: Where in the Organization Can Leaders Grow?

Chapter 15: Associate   105

Chapter 16: Manager   111

Chapter 17: Director   119

Chapter 18: Vice President   129

Chapter 19: Chief Level   139

SECTION FIVE: How Should You Develop Leaders?

Chapter 20: Demonstrate   153

Chapter 21: Delegate   161

Chapter 22: Motivate   167

Chapter 23: Operate   173

SECTION SIX: Leadership That Lasts

Chapter 24: Create   181

Chapter 25: Regulate   187

Chapter 26: Accelerate   193

Chapter 27: Future State   201

Chapter 28: Triplicate   211

Notes   221

About the Author   229

Preface

The foremost subject of interest throughout my life has been leadership. From an early age, I recognized the power and possibility of leading others toward a shared outcome. I recall the first time a leader at my church suggested that I could help lead a group. It was humbling and I had much to learn, but since then, I've never stopped thinking about what makes leaders better and more effective. I've grown to understand that the greater the collective benefit from achieving that shared outcome, the greater the opportunity to engage and secure commitment from others.

Since that early age, I've evolved from immature and self-absorbed aspirations of getting people to do what I wanted them to do, to galvanizing teams around an energizing vision and outcomes that are good for all. The change in thinking began simply, moving from begging my parents for a particular toy that I wanted to collaborating with my siblings to strategize ways to get our parents to let us stay up later. It was a good journey from fighting to get that toy so no one else could get it to working collectively to help our parents understand our viewpoint.

It's a small example of how much more enjoyable it is to work as a team toward a positive shared outcome. I had fun figuring out leadership skills and how to use them, even as a youth. I observed my teachers in classrooms, coaches on fields and courts, and political leaders on television. I thought about their techniques and level of effectiveness. I studied the behaviors and the decisions of coaches who won multiple championships and listened to their post-game press conferences. I read the newspaper articles afterward to see what they had to say about their win. I even reflected on the public's responses to the coaches' comments. I thought about the ways that the coaches' comments affected their athletes' thoughts and perceptions of the game, their coach, and their team.

I studied business leaders' public comments and then paid attention to my experience as a consumer, interacting with their brands to find alignment or disconnect. These activities provided me with insights about whether their leadership methodologies were just words or whether the principles were truly apparent in the culture of the organization. I read books about their organizations and their leadership approaches to glean whatever I could to have examples—good or bad—that I could leverage and apply in my own leadership journey.

I studied religious and political historical leaders—those who led revolutions, those who received a calling from God, and even the stories of unassuming people who were thrust into leadership roles at an early age or later in life when they hadn't expected or asked for it. I looked for consistent threads woven through the leadership fabric of these vastly different lives of people who lived long before my lifetime but whose stories were well preserved and are still told today. I took away perspectives from the widely different materials and content—history books, biographies, the Bible, leadership books—all yielding different insights about how leaders used their talents and skills and

Preface

illuminating how the authors and storytellers perceived their leadership and preserved the lessons learned.

At age thirteen, I got my first paid job and began to experience and think about leadership styles, effectiveness, and outcomes in the workplace. Whether I was working for leaders at for-profit organizations, not-for-profit organizations, or even just enjoying different social settings, I was drawn to observe leadership styles in different life contexts. I watched supervisors, teachers, and coaches and gleaned learnings from each of them. I've always been fascinated by the practice of leadership and the ways it affects people, groups, and organizations.

Regardless of our context or circumstances and irrespective of our age, educational attainment, gender, race, culture, or our perceptions and motivations, everyone, at some time or other, will witness or experience good leaders and bad leaders. There are always great successes because of great leadership, and sometimes there are bad outcomes even with great leadership. It is even possible for bad leaders to get good results, and, of course, they might get bad outcomes as a result of their poor leadership. However, on balance, over time, great leaders far outperform bad or even average leaders. The odds favor great leaders, which begs the question: What makes a great leader?

At moments in this book, you'll notice that I reference three populations: you, the leader who wants to develop others and the core audience for this book; the potential leader(s) you aim to develop as leaders; and finally, the organizations where you serve and lead. It is my hope that this book will accomplish two things. First, you will know a few traits of great leaders. While this book is written for those who are leading now and want to develop other leaders, you might be just beginning your leadership journey and aspire to be a great leader. You can work to apply these principles to your life, not only for your benefit but also for the benefit of those you lead. The second objective—benefiting others—is a much more difficult task, but it is the purpose and design of this book—to help leaders develop other leaders intentionally and authentically.

You'll find that I lean on historical and biblical examples that I think have had success promulgating true, multigenerational leadership development. As a result, those organizations have endured, and their purposes have been sustained for many years. Most organizations are not sustainable, and within a few years become a mere shell of themselves or, even worse, are nonexistent. Some research suggests that the average organizational lifespan of companies on Standard and Poor's 500 Index is currently about twenty years.[1] I think that a contributing factor to the quick rise and fall of organizations, and their failure to sustain their work and purpose, is due to failed leadership.

I suppose it's unsurprising that business lifespans are so short-lived, since history shows that all kingdoms fall. The greatest civilizations in history, and many nation states and regimes, have risen and fallen. Some took hundreds of years to finally fail, and others fell quickly; therein lies the premise for this book. While I don't expect that we who lead organizations today are likely to build an enduring institution that necessarily rivals the impact and staying power of these United States of America (soon to reach 250 years old), and certainly cannot replicate the growth and endurance of the Christian church—the other multigenerational institution that I'll often reference—I do believe that we can improve our ability to develop leaders who are well prepared and who are inspired by a shared vision and outcomes that in turn result in more sustainable, enduring organizations. My love for history brought me to the leadership of George Washington. Washington unselfishly declined a salary for his military service during the Revolutionary War and attempted to decline a salary as president; however, the law requires it, and Congress insisted that he accept one.[2] Later, Washington willingly exited his role as president, choosing not to seek a third term. These early decisions helped ensure that leadership was continual and uninterrupted and that the purpose of creating an enduring constitutional republic was secured.

As a Christian, I've also studied the life and leadership of Jesus. His teachings and parables have shaped the way I understand people and leadership, and the Bible is a treasure trove of stories and experiences that have helped shape and form my life, leadership, and learning. Jesus's leadership of His core twelve followers serves as a model for leadership development and was the instrument for moving His message and purpose forward and helped ensure that His church endured through the ages.

At the heart of these two examples of impactful leadership is the intent to safeguard a meaningful purpose.

Leaders who are intent on inviting others to be part of a larger purpose are inspiring and their institutions more sustainable. I once heard a coach say, "I've learned that I'm a better coach when I have better players." I found that statement a little funny. It seems obvious that the coach's job is easier when they have superstar players who help them win games. In context, he was suggesting that his success—measured by the number of wins and losses—was more assured when he had top talent. However, talent alone is not what it takes to build a successful program. Great coaching that develops leaders on and off the field ensures all potential is maximized, making the outcomes the organization seeks more assured.

It is rare to find teams or organizations that focus on developing other leaders, resulting in multigenerational continuity and success. I enjoy taking time to learn about those special leaders. I enjoy sports, so, of course, I've reviewed the lives and practices of coaches who've led their teams to championships. Many coaches who've earned championship wins are not able to replicate their success. Most don't experience success over multiple decades, and most do not have an heir apparent to ensure that the organization, and the people who are a part of it, continues to experience success long after the leader exits the organization.

A key indicator of great leadership could be that an organization grows and thrives for many decades or even for generations after a leader is no longer in their role or is no longer alive. The only way to make this work, in my experience, is to develop a culture of leadership development that invests in leaders who will then invest in other leaders.

If you are currently a leader, I believe part of your job is to develop other leaders. This book is for you. The aim of this book is to provide a primer on leadership development that includes principles and frameworks for helping to develop effective leaders. Strong leaders are foundational to building enduring organizations that span many decades and experience multigenerational successes. When successful cycles of leadership development are in place, individual lives, families, institutions, communities, and even nations are better and healthier for the investment. These are principles and frameworks I've relied upon and refined in my own business to identify and develop leaders who know and understand the organization's purpose and vision and who have the requisite skills to invest in others who take the baton and carry it forward. Such replicable success is accomplished only by developing leaders who develop other leaders in an ongoing, intentional, and predictable way. Without such principles and processes in place for leadership development, long-term success of any organization is tenuous at best. This book is designed to help you get there. It will be a challenge, as success is multifactorial and never guaranteed. Many have tried, and while a few have created enduring organizations, history says that most have not.

If you're a reader who has not yet assumed a leadership role in a defined or formal way, but you aim to be one someday, may I suggest that you begin with self-reflection about your unique talent and capacity for leadership, and before you hop into leading others, figure out your own unique purpose? I recommend that you start by reading my first book, *Transform through Purpose: Your Path to Living an Authentic and Intentional Life*, to determine your life priorities, create habits that will enable you to honor your priorities, and then discover and start living your life *of* purpose *on* purpose. Become the person with potential who other leaders notice. Become a strong candidate for leadership development.

In my view, leading well includes developing other leaders. Your role as a leader doesn't stop with motivating people, managing projects, or directing processes. Your role as a leader extends to pursuing and promoting the purpose of your people and your organization. Being an intentional leader who develops the next generation of leaders carries that purpose forward. I hope you can work toward a purpose that matters and that you want to see endure for a long time.

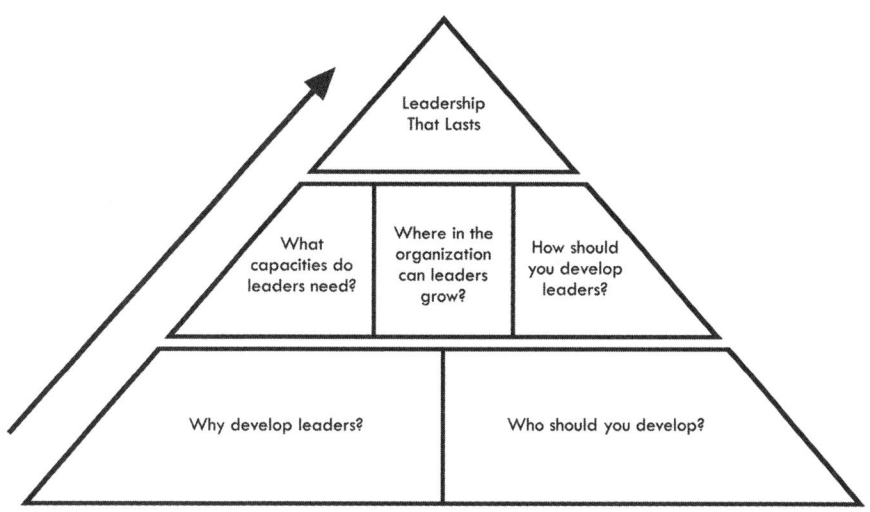

Lead Exponentially

LEAD EXPONENTIALLY

This book includes some of my own learnings and experience leading a growing global security franchising firm based in Omaha, Nebraska. I hope that when you complete this book you have a stronger understanding of the role and importance of leadership and have some insights and skills into the principles and frameworks to share with aspiring leaders who are committed to leading in their families, organizations, communities, the country, and the world. I hope you will help other leaders learn ways to ensure that the places they care most about persist and do not fall but continue to be places for people to live purposeful lives. Begin to lead exponentially and help propel those leaders into their best future. Because the future rests with them.

—REED

SECTION ONE

Why Develop Leaders?

Let's begin thinking about the work of identifying and developing leaders by unpacking the *why* that underlies the calling. I believe that developing leaders can be considered a calling rather than a task or even a role. A *calling* implies that the work serves a purpose beyond yourself. As you invest in others, you expand the capacity of individuals and whole organizations to navigate the uncertainties of the future, creating something that lasts beyond yourself.

Thinking about why you should identify and develop leaders ensures that your purpose is rooted firmly in the right things. Researchers are tasked with stating the purpose of their project. Business owners and nonprofit founders craft mission and vision statements that help codify their why and communicate the purpose for their work. Similarly, as a leader who wants to develop others, you should reflect on why you choose to invest in specific individuals, so you may be intentional with your approach.

While there are many great reasons to develop leaders, I'd like you to consider these four: First, you ensure that talent is not wasted by maximizing demonstrated **potential** of others; next, you prioritize **experiential** elements of your organization by recognizing the influence of leaders to mold them; third, by investing in leaders, you enable **exponential** growth and improvement of people and the organization; and finally, by developing other leaders, you assume a **beneficial** role that values identifying and meeting the needs of others today and in the future.

CHAPTER 1

Potential

Knowing why you select individuals to develop is the first step. Leaders have accountability and responsibility for helping people maximize their full potential. When this happens, it is good for everyone. Regardless of whom you decide to develop and what the ultimate outcome is, the goal is that people are better, more confident leaders. You do not develop leaders for your own benefit but for their benefit. Leaders who believe it is their calling to identify and develop other leaders with purpose and intentionality help create thriving families, communities, workplaces, and organizations, and people's lives are better for it.

Look for Leadership Talent

Identifying and developing the right people for leadership can be challenging because there is only so much time and energy available. I have provided guidance, support, and encouragement to many people who wanted to improve their leadership skills and who said they wanted to make a difference. I've had individuals ask me directly to give them an opportunity to grow in their leadership skills, but some research suggests that only about one in ten people have the requisite talent—the natural ability for excellence—for people management.[1] Therefore, it's important to identify and develop people well for any level of leadership they might eventually assume.

I've observed over the years that people aspire to lead others for a variety of reasons. Some aim for increased pay or to attain a specific role or title. Others aim to have more responsibility or to learn new things. I've found there are a few possible outcomes for those who attain some level of leadership in an organization. Sometimes the individual was not ready to be a leader. Some fail to grow or progress once they achieve that desired role, title, or salary. They are satisfied with the changes they experienced and seem to hit a leadership ceiling, and sometimes that happens after just a short time. Then there are others who claim that the ceiling on their growth as a leader was due to their circumstances or the environment, and that might be the case. The environment can certainly introduce barriers to progress and growth for current and potential leaders.

Another possible outcome of investing in leaders who demonstrate potential is that the individual reaches the point where the learner surpasses the teacher in understanding and practice. Some leaders exhibit a level of ingenuity and persistence that allows them to forge new pathways forward. Leaders you develop might be able to make the culture and the people around them better, and, eventually, they might need to find a different environment with the guidance of a different leader to continue to develop and grow. In a small way, I experienced this as a coach of my children's sports teams. I was able to help them improve by teaching them some fundamentals of their respective sport, and I could give them some basics of being a supportive teammate. However, about the time they hit junior high school, their coaching needs and their capacity as athletes surpassed my capacity as a coach. So, it was fun to move them on to their various clubs and school teams where they could continue to grow as athletes and team leaders. Similarly, in your business or organization, there may be talented individuals with potential beyond the opportunities that your organization is able to provide for them. Be willing to facilitate their success in another environment. It can be tough to do, but cheer them on as they go! Those alumni leaders might serve as brand ambassadors for your organization, if you support their exit with intentionality and care.[2]

A fourth possible outcome of identifying and developing people with leadership potential is that they grow and eventually succeed you as a leader. This outcome might be most rare, and it requires some of the best leaders, with an exceptionally well-choreographed process, time, and effort to develop a leader to that stage. Developing leaders is about stewarding and propelling the purpose of the organization forward into the future. It is about investing in others' potential so they and the organization can be their best. Regrettably, few organizations and leaders have this kind of purposeful leadership development in mind, however.

I appreciate historical examples of generational, transformative leadership—leadership that helps a purpose to endure. The first unanimously elected president of the United States, George Washington, willingly transferred executive leadership of the country to the next leader—a critical moment that helped the young nation state endure. Challenges, both internal and external, to the United States have been myriad over the decades, but by the time this book is published, it will have endured for nearly 250 years, thanks, in part, to the successful transition of leadership to other leaders in those formative decades.

Take Notice

In organizations, sometimes potential goes unnoticed in favor of those who are the top draft pics or valedictorians of their class, for example. However, these top performers may not always be the best leaders or developers of leaders in the long term. They do not always end up being Hall of Famers in a leadership development context. Sometimes it is necessary to look more carefully for the leadership potential that could be developed for the future. Find those who are the best fit for the mission, the role, or the team. With the right kind of opportunity, they could lead and help fulfill your organization's purpose. Many potential leaders reach a pinnacle too soon in their work and growth because no one took the time to invest in them. That potential is left untapped. Keep a keen eye out for those talented people who could realize their potential with intentional time and development. See, notice, and acknowledge their potential, even—or especially—if they do not yet see it themselves.

As you begin to identify the leadership potential in people, look for ways that their unique characteristics manifest themselves. Maybe people tend to gravitate toward them or maybe their disposition is one that easily fosters trust. Their potential should be apparent, but it may, of course, be unrefined. You might notice that their potential is demonstrated in a variety of different circumstances, or perhaps it is demonstrated consistently, over time, within one context. They may easily befriend others or be able to communicate clearly and transparently. They may have the ability to positively influence others, or they may make consistently good decisions. With your support, they could further develop their potential. Whatever talent you observe, you should see potential that can grow along with your organization.

CHAPTER 2

Experiential

Another reason for identifying and developing leaders is because of the experiences that capable leaders create for others around them. Leaders influence and mold experiential elements of your organization. Strong leaders help create an environment where people want to live, learn, and work. They have a disposition that helps others feel valued and heard. You want to identify high potential leaders and develop them so that they will celebrate others' successes and find ways to multiply them.

An Eye on the End Game

Some of the best group experiences I've had were when the group had a clear vision, and everyone was working well together toward a common goal. Roles were clearly defined, and the hand-selected team worked toward the outcome, and everyone was aligned. This combination is generally a recipe for success. One time, however, this amazing team combination technically ended in a loss, but the whole season was truly a leadership win.

When I was in college, I played on an intramural soccer team. I never played soccer in high school, so the last time I had played was in elementary school. However, a couple of my friends were playing and said they needed a goalie for their team. I was a wrestler in high school, and I was accustomed to facing tough and challenging opponents, so despite my lack of soccer experience, I tried out and made the team. It was quickly obvious that I was the least experienced member of that soccer team, but the team captain was a strong leader. He made it fun and helped us remain focused on the upcoming competitions and knew what we needed to do to get ready. He was well prepared and had a clear focus on outcomes for our team. He had a strong understanding of positions needed and planned accordingly. It mattered not whether we were ahead or behind in the games; he remained focused on the next opportunity, play, or potential goal.

If our team fell behind or did not execute well one week, he assigned the blame to himself and his failure to make the right coaching decisions at the right times. We had a great season and made it to the championship game. We fell one win short of an intramural championship and finished as runners-up in the league. We surpassed our collective potential, and it was one of the best sports experiences I've ever had, despite not coming out on top. It was only the intramural league, and I was not even a strong player. But the leader saw my potential, coached me in the right techniques, and helped me get better. We created many great memories, and I took away many lessons in teamwork and leadership that I still lean on decades later.

Experiential

Positive, Others-Centered Culture

As you are identifying leaders with potential, be sure that they value the experiences they create for others within their sphere of influence. They understand that the final outcomes are byproducts of the experiences they create, and if they are incessantly focused on the outcome to the neglect of the experience, those outcomes may be less likely to come to fruition. And the process—not only the final product or outcome—is such a critical part of growth and development. Perhaps you've seen an organization that—on paper—has all the talent and resources they need to do great things, but, nonetheless, the team is fractured or unfocused and they fail to realize their potential. This is sometimes a result of poor culture. A poor culture is the result of cumulative experiences that stymie rather than cultivate excellence. Leaders are responsible for crafting those experiences. If the adage oft attributed to Peter Drucker is correct, and culture does indeed "eat strategy for breakfast," then you must identify potential leaders who value humans and create unity around a shared purpose.[1]

Leaders who are focused on creating positive experiences for their teams know that the most meaningful successes are crafted in environments where all members feel valued for their strengths and contributions. Disrespect is toxic to organizations, and it is especially destructive if facilitated—or ignored—by leaders.[2] In every interaction, it is critical to help others know that their perspectives and experiences matter. While leaders cannot always adopt suggestions or advice from everyone, they should practice listening to others' vantage point.

As you spot potential and begin to identify and develop leaders, model the kind of experience they should learn to create. Create a positive development experience that makes them inclined to learn and grow more. I've had times when I've seen leadership potential in someone, so I've attempted to invest in that potential, only to have them question and complain along the way. Sometimes they've even proceeded in the opposite direction, only to return to ask for help to address the ensuing challenges that arose from not heeding the advice! It's awkward, of course, and the outcome is generally disappointing. When the wrong leaders are leading, the environment and experiences they create drive good talent away. They tend to suck the air out of a room. Some find it difficult to practice the humility necessary to create an experience that others—both leaders and followers—want to participate in.

I have a colleague whom I invited as a leader at our organization. I knew him from our church. He let me know he was wanting to develop and learn as a leader, so I encouraged him to begin his own group at church. He did. He began practicing and is a valued leader of my team today. Potential can grow and be refined in a variety of settings. People can build leadership capacity at work, at home, and in their communities.

Mixing It Up

As I think about identifying and developing a leader, I look for potential that is demonstrated in one or more areas of their lives. Sometimes it is difficult to understand and spot potential in a singular context and may not be fully representative of their capacity and potential. I also consider the experiences they create for themselves and others. I enjoy figuring out the ways they lead and serve in different environments and the kinds of experiences they create for others. I recently began a selection process to add leaders to my team. I created a multistep, multiday process to help provide access to different parts of our organization.

The process began with a job posting that highlighted different aspects of the role. I interviewed several candidates, asking questions consistently to gauge different kinds of responses, which is always interesting and enlightening. While some résumés and backgrounds for some candidates seemed similar, the way that they approached and answered questions and the way they dialogued, was, of course, different. We interviewed approximately one hundred people in that initial phase, then invited twenty of them to the next phase; fifteen of them agreed to continue to the next step, but just eleven showed and participated. The four who opted out seemed to realize the organization was not a right fit for them and their specific aspirations. One of the elements I was screening for was the ways that their interactions could create a positive experience for me and others. The finalists participated in a two-day interview process, rotating through four or five group interviews with ten to twelve potential coworkers. They also participated in a few social events and met a couple of our clients.

Throughout the group interviews, formal and informal meetings, and social events, the various strengths of each candidate became clearer. Some had well-crafted responses to questions, others were very comfortable in an array of business and social contexts and conversations. Having an array of meetings and opportunities helped inform the selection process. It was important to home in on the candidate that, overall, could be a strong contributor and decision-maker in an array of settings and with diverse teams.

Ultimately, I made an offer to a few of the candidates, outlining the desired outcomes for their role. My intent is to avoid the pitfalls that sometimes come for those who want a title rather than embracing the responsibilities of being a leader. Those who were invited to join the organization demonstrated consistently positive experiences, which they themselves helped to create, in a variety of different contexts. Each of the candidates had strong interactions and the capacity to interact and relate with potential colleagues and customers. The expanded approach for our interviews can be taxing and requires a good bit of time on behalf of our team members, and the candidates, but, ultimately, it helped get a preview of the potential fit of the individual within our organization. Leaders must recognize that they are in their role to serve others and help them achieve their goals.

As you identify and develop leaders within an enduring leadership tree that has branches and fruit multiplied across your organization, ensure those leaders can craft experiences that attract and support people, the purpose, and the outcomes. Look at the experiences they create on a small scale within a small group or team setting and in formal and informal settings. Many people select talent based on previous job titles and roles, and sometimes it can be difficult to gauge the extent to which they have supported positive outcomes within those roles. Try to find scenarios where you can witness the tangible and intangible contributions leaders make for others. Choosing a leader who creates consistently bad experiences for themselves and for others will be difficult to change. Your own time is finite. Ensure that it is spent developing leaders who create positive experiences for others.

CHAPTER 3

Exponential

Another reason for identifying and developing leaders is to facilitate the long-term, exponential growth of both the person and the organization. Leaders who understand how to multiply talent, knowledge, and skills help spur growth by ensuring that decision-making is distributed widely, reducing the numbers and kinds of speed bumps that arise. As you develop leaders, you invariably multiply the growth and success of individuals and teams, which ultimately creates a stable, healthy organization. Leaders who are focused on others rather than their own gain scatter seeds from their learnings, which sprout and grow within the lives of others.

Again, how easy it would have been for George Washington to hoard the power he earned. But instead, he was self-sacrificing in his leadership. He was known for his capacity to engender trust and lead others throughout the grim years of the American Revolution and was unanimously elected the first president of the United States, in 1789. He voluntarily resigned his commission as commander-in-chief of the Continental Army following the signing of the Treaty of Paris in 1783, and his commitment to the founding purpose of the nation opened the way for subsequent leaders to pick up the baton and steer the nation, resulting in a stable transfer of power and leadership.[1]

Dividing and Multiplying

You may have experienced events or conferences where you left feeling more depleted in energy, time, or resources than energized and ready to tackle a next challenge or opportunity. These experiences feel draining and are not sustainable in the long term. Inevitably, when you have repeated interactions where you feel that energy and optimism are absent, division, disagreement, and discontent can settle in. There may need to be an exit strategy, a proactive separation, or some other divide-to-grow approach. This could be a way to avoid ongoing distraction and help to maintain the organization's focus and progress.

When we moved into our first home, my wife, Dana, and I were trying to make choices for our landscaping. Since neither of us have a green thumb, we needed low-maintenance perennials that could stand up to the Midwest winters. We also wanted something that would provide a pop of color. When we entered the showroom, we were quickly directed to the daylilies. They were just what we were looking for: There were many colors to choose from, they are resistant to the periodically extreme temperature shifts, and they could grow and fill the space in our flower beds. It was going to be tough, though, to stay within our budget and fill the large space we had with plants. The representative let us know that daylilies can thrive when they are split. They advised us to plant them and then the next year cut them in half and replant them. With good air, water, sun, soil, and a little patience, they would grow, and in just a few years, the split plants would be larger than the original plants. I was confounded by that idea, but it was true! And I find it to be such a strong metaphor for relationships and organizations.

I was accustomed to having seeds that grow into plants that are unique and grow when nurtured. The notion of these plants doubling in size after being split challenged my thinking about ideas and business. I thought each idea had a unique starting point that was planted and nurtured. And then it would bloom and drop a new and different seed that would give life for the next idea. But the idea that a healthy plant could grow more by being divided instead of dying when it is cut in half and replanted was an interesting new potential analogy that resonated with me. It happens that other plants, besides daylilies, are equally as resilient. Mint, I've since learned, is another plant that can be cut and replanted and grow exponentially. My friend plants a backyard vegetable garden every year and planted mint once. The next year, he didn't plant mint, but nonetheless, it showed up in the garden box because it's so resilient. (If you've got a green thumb, I'm sure you can appreciate my delight in these discoveries!)

It was contrary to my perception that things cannot live if something is always taken away from them. However, some things can thrive when they are divided or separated. This is true for some plants, but I think it can also be true for people and organizations. It's fun, for example, to see the connections that exist between elite coaches. Coaches have assistants who learn, then often leave to lead elsewhere. While there are coaches with more prolific coaching trees, currently Andy Reid, head coach of the Kansas City Chiefs, has the largest active coaching tree, consisting of five former assistants who currently lead NFL teams, as of this writing.[2] In addition to the recently earned Super Bowl wins, he has left his stamp on NFL franchise leadership for years to come. His coaching leadership has grown and spread in and through other coaches.

Grow for a Purpose

Find leaders who recognize the need for and power of this exponential view of growth and enduring purpose. They should be open to change and see chances for exploring a new environment or context to support growth. When strong leaders go to a new place, they can leave and replant their talent and life elsewhere to pursue a new vision or idea. They take their learnings, experiences, and maybe even resources that can support growth in a new way and in a new place. Leading and growing should never stop; they should spread. They should be shared in ways that could be exponentially meaningful.

Identifying and developing leaders who can spread your organization's purpose and ultimately bring in success—maybe even outside of the organization—is very rewarding. Adding a strong contributor has a tremendous additive effect for the organization, but when you find a leader who can bring out the best in others, and then multiply their lessons and leadership, that has opportunity to bring exponential value for many people and the organization. Such exponential value in developing strong leaders is akin to saving dollars versus investing them, which can yield an even greater long-term return. Multiplying talent and effort via training, coaching, and peer mentoring ensures that skills, knowledge, and talent are leveraged strategically and the opportunity for success is maximized.

As I've shared, faith is my first and most critical life priority. As a Christian, I'm greatly influenced by Jesus's life and ministry. I'm fascinated by the people Jesus selected and invited to participate with Him during His earthly ministry. Most were young, but He saw their potential and their willingness to serve and lead, even though they were people others may not have chosen or even noticed. Jesus had a close group of twelve disciples whom He invested in, and while other followers surrounded His ministry, these men listened and learned and were among the apostles sent to grow the church among the nations. Simon (also called Peter) and Andrew, for example, immediately left their fishing nets when Jesus called to them, saying, "Come follow me, and I will show you how to fish for people!"[3] They immediately left their nets—their livelihood—to follow Him and learn from Him and to do what He did.[4] The disciples' willing apprenticeship was foundational to helping the Christian faith endure and grow over the millennia.

The US, as a constitutional republic, is an example of distributed power and leadership, while maintaining a central identity. The states are entrusted with power to establish their own structure of governance, under leadership of a governor and legislature, while also having representation in the federal government. Of course, the success of the nation was contingent on the success of the states, as the founders worked to strike the careful balance of power with overlapping interests for the states. The leadership in the country is simultaneously decentralized and centralized—a balance that has ebbed and flowed throughout the decades. If you look at countries that have adopted a democracy model with large amounts of power held at the state or province level, they are in many instances larger on a per-capita GDP basis than those with any other form of governance. But that is certainly not the only defining characteristic for success, as personal well-being and happiness,[5] for example, are other important measures of thriving.

As you identify and develop leaders, seek those who understand the value of growing exponentially, who will both champion and share the organization's purpose, and who will immediately begin to invest in the lives of others to help share and grow that purpose. There is a distinct difference between those who are outstanding individual contributors in an organization, who can handle a volume of tasks and complete them excellently, and those who are ready to lead these excellent contributors. High performers, who produce a lot and do their work well, are invaluable to an organization's success and growth. However, finding these talented people is different than inviting leaders who are able to make connections, spot leadership potential in others, and then make decisions and changes that put those leaders in positions to help grow the organization exponentially. This kind of leadership has potential to not only be additive for the organization but to help nurture growth and success through many seasons. Great athletes, for example, do not necessarily make the best coaches. And many athletes who were not necessarily the top stars of their team may have the talent required to be great coaches. The best leaders unlock the potential of others to pursue and champion the purpose. They do this by analyzing an array of factors that can help set their team members up for individual and collective success. They relentlessly pursue that success, while keeping an eye on the vision of the organization. Identify and develop leaders so they can help unite around the purpose and facilitate exponential growth of individuals, teams, and organizations.

CHAPTER 4

Beneficial

Finally, it is important to identify and develop leaders because of the role they assume to provide for and benefit others. They give individuals and team members what they need in critical moments and, in the long run, ensure they can do their work and overcome barriers. Leaders aim to provide a better life and secure future—one that they themselves might not even get a chance to see! They have a strong future orientation, as will be described later, and they hope that their investment of time, energy, talent, and skills will create a healthy and enduring environment for subsequent generations.

Privileged to Provide

Again, the reason investing in leaders is so critical is because of their role to provide for and benefit others. Leaders should wake up each day thinking about the future that they want to create and know what they must provide for others who are a part of that future. Strong leaders help create and provide stability in their organizations. They aim to provide environments where generations of people can grow.

Leaders who understand their role is to provide for the benefit of others aim to create places that endure rather than succumbing to deceptive strategies that promise temporal success. The world is, quite literally, littered with those who want this kind of quick return. We are a society filled with consumers, and while consumption is a key driver in our capitalist system, it is critical to produce and provide in sustainable ways. As the rate of growth of the United States' GDP is blunted, and the national debt climbs higher, evidence mounts that we are not planning to provide for others generationally; leaders are making short-term decisions rather than providing for the future. They focus on present satisfaction rather than seeking long-term fulfillment, and it will be costly for future generations.

Pitfalls of Short-Term Thinking

If you are intent on developing leaders, you may find that some talented, capable leaders are driven by self-interest and immediate rewards and gains. Identify and develop leaders with shared belief in sustainable leadership. Develop those who can build an enduring legacy over the long term.

Intentionally develop leaders because leaders leave a legacy and, too often, it is a poor one. For too many unsuccessful companies and organizations, their ultimate collapse was due to short-term-thinking and self-interested leaders who sabotaged success. They did not create sustainable organizations that provide well-being and opportunity for generations to come. Rather, greed and self-interest drove their actions.

Enron, WorldCom, and, more recently, Theranos, are just a few examples of massive individual and corporate greed that now fuels whole seasons' worth of television programs.

In some manufacturing settings, I think there has been a pivot away from producing high-quality products that last a long time to a goal of selling more stuff that can generate revenue most quickly. Right out of college, I went to work for BLACK+DECKER's power tools division. The company had built a solid brand over several decades but had experienced a shrink in market share. There was a perception among leadership that consumers had become confused about the differences between the quality standards of tools built for consumers versus professional-grade tools.

The company decided to work to position a premium brand of tools. They went to many sawmills and always saw DeWalt brand machines from the 1950s, and they were still operating. It is impressive that those saws had likely made hundreds or thousands of cuts, but they just never failed or needed replacing. In 1960, DeWalt was sold to BLACK+DECKER and underwent a brand refresh, positioning "DeWalt as the high-end brand and BLACK+DECKER as the brand for consumers."[1] The model was like that of the auto industry, which marketed different brand tiers for different consumer perceptions and needs. When you visit sources on the history of DeWalt, you'll see their commitment to excellence highlighted. I think it is true regardless of the product, whether it is a mid-twentieth-century DeWalt saw or a deep freeze your grandmother has owned for several decades: For many years there was an intent by manufacturing companies to build products that would stand the test of time. Short-term thinkers with strong self-interest to drive revenue and profits might conspire to lower those quality standards for products or services, increasing the need for servicing to generate more revenue and push consumers to purchase products more frequently. But such short-term thinking is not a sustainable path and does not result in a stable, enduring organization.

It is imperative that leaders choose the better, more sustainable path. The health of our organizations, our communities, and our world depends on it. You must identify and develop leaders intentionally and help them avoid the temptation of self-interested, short-term decision-making that will ultimately lead to losses, result in elevated downstream costs to the organization, and prevent the capacity of your organization to provide for generations to come.

The auto industry has had fluctuations around its commitment to quality engineering and manufacturing. The interesting thing for me is that today there are many avid car restorers and collectors. There is a whole economy built around buying, restoring, and showing vintage vehicles that stand the test of time. The investment of time, artistry, engineering, and skill helps extend the longevity and the value of those mid-century masterpieces that others can now appreciate. Providing products and services that help an organization persist and provide benefit over time is worth pursuing.

Content to Serve

Leaders who understand their job is to provide for others for their benefit also understand that making long-term decisions matters. Identify and find those who relish providing for others' needs. Sometimes this can be observed in simple behaviors. I observe the small things. If they are walking into a building, do they tend to hold the door open for others, taking just a little time to provide a service for someone else? Do they notice the needs of others around them, and are they inclined to offer help or support, even if there is not a particular reason to do so or an obvious benefit for them? If they tend to provide for the needs

Beneficial

of others in the small things, I find there's a good chance they will be inclined to make decisions that provide for the good of others and the organization around the big things. At Virginia Tech University, the motto is *Ut Prosim*, "That I may serve." A small demonstration of this is that students hold the doors open for others, typically—a small gesture that is a peek into a culture where people think about what others need.

Not only do you look for behaviors that illustrate the ways your leader candidates provide for the needs of others, but you must also listen to their words and language. Identify and develop leaders who seem to be good listeners and ask good questions. While some people have good words and can keep our interest and have wisdom, those with an aim for meeting others' needs are often skilled at inviting responses. Talking is not unimportant, but asking questions brings another level of thoughtfulness. Skilled listening and focusing on others rather than oneself is one small indicator that someone might embrace their role as a leader who provides for others. A well-crafted question provides good insight into the things that people are curious about. Skilled trial lawyers are often masters of the art and science of crafting and asking good questions. They spend many hours preparing for the trial, pouring over mounds of evidence and sorting the most critical details while also spending many hours and resources to craft the questions that are designed to evoke responses that boost the chances of winning their case. Similarly, it is important to develop leaders who can design questions that can build their understanding, ignite passion, and ultimately, help drive all parties in a positive direction and toward a positive outcome.

As an early leader, I was inclined to make statements to colleagues and teams, assuming people understood and were committed to the initiative or idea I'd presented. If a new leader asked a question or wanted advice about what to do, I was quick to provide a directive.

Later, I learned to entrust more decisions to the leader. I once had a high-potential leader join our organization who asked me for some specific direction about an issue. Early in my career, I would have gladly provided the directive and next steps. Instead, I responded that I trusted they would figure out the best solution to the issue and asked what help and resources they needed to design that solution. That moment of entrusting the leader to do the work and supporting with resources was a good learning moment for us both.

I'm reminded of the many holiday meals that my family has had together. When we arrive at a family member's house, I ask what and when questions: "What's for dinner?" and "When will dinner be ready?" Whereas, my aunt often arrives and immediately asks, "How can I help with the meal?" My questions are squarely centered on what I want and need. Her question is centered on my grandmother and others who do the work and what they need. I listen for ways that service-minded people ask questions and how they center the needs of other people in those questions.

The Little Things Matter

In addition to looking at behaviors that demonstrate a capacity to provide for the benefit of others and listening to words and questions that center others, I also consider their lives and ways that they've demonstrated providing for others. There is always evidence of a life well lived on behalf of others. The daily decisions to provide for the needs of others and center them with our words and behaviors will generally be consistent, regardless of context, for others who have the capacity to be leaders. People who are intent on meeting others' needs will do so at work, at home, and/or in their community. The compilation of deeds—not just words—is a strong indicator of whether they understand the role of leaders is to provide for and benefit others. Those decisions and actions must align with the words said.

Take note of whether the leaders you identify to develop have evidence across many areas of their life that they are intent on providing for others in the long term. Consider whether they prioritize their own self-interest or whether they truly are looking to provide better experiences for others.

Select leaders and develop them with an aim to create an enduring, sustainable organization that builds well-being for individuals and the community for the long haul. You will have a better chance at creating a culture in your organization that maximizes potential, is defined by meaningful and positive experiences, grows its purpose and work exponentially, and benefits others by developing leaders who exhibit these in their lives and have them as their defining values and motivators. Reflect on these four areas to understand why developing leaders is critical, and you will be better at helping leaders maximize their potential over time.

Failing to select the right people can stunt your organization's growth, so let's think more about who you should develop.

SECTION TWO

Who Should You Develop?

Now that you have a foundation for understanding why it is critical to identify and develop leaders, you must think more about who you should develop. I suggest that the leaders you identify and develop should possess **character, charisma, and commitment**, and they should be **collaborative and connected** with others.

CHAPTER 5

Character

I've shared that my top priority in life is my faith. I've chosen to follow Jesus and been a Christian for many years. One reason I placed my faith in Jesus is because He lived a sinless life. The words He preached and the principles He taught are powerful, and yet they resonate with millions of people because of His authentic goodness demonstrated through His actions. He did not possess wealth but was a humble carpenter, and as the Son of God, lived a perfect life, teaching and loving others. Because He faithfully lived out the principles of His Kingdom, His Gospel message matched His actions. He prioritized the weak. Humbled the proud. He shared meals and interacted with sinners, and offered forgiveness, freedom, and healing. He noticed those whom others didn't see. Had there been a character flaw or obvious disconnect between the way He lived and what He preached, I suggest that His life and ministry might well have been invalidated, and the church might not have grown and persisted through time. Very regrettably, many leaders who've claimed to be followers of Jesus have done incalculable damage to the cause and mission of Christ because their lives do not reflect His character. Jesus sent and empowered the church to preach the Gospel in the power of His Spirit and His followers. Leaders of the church are to develop and model their thinking and their lives after His.[1] He is my example of living a life of character.

Character Still Counts Most

I suggest you identify and develop leaders who have demonstrated strong, unwavering character. Not original to me, of course, but I think "character" is simply who one is when no one is looking. The implication is that the words and deeds of someone who has strong character are consistent, whether others see and observe those words or deeds or not. Character is not performative.

I fear that the standards of strong character and morality in our country have been weakened. Data suggests I'm not alone in that perception. A 2021 Gallup Poll showed nearly half of US adults say the overall state of moral values in this country is "poor" compared with just 1 percent who say it is excellent.[2] Such an environment where values and morality are uncertain is a recipe for mistrust and fear to abound.

There are too many examples in our society where leaders—and others—have failed to live up to the standards of character that are required and needed. I fear that these publicized examples threaten to shift our belief in the abiding value of strong character. If the target for what defines strong and trustworthy character is unreliable and movable, again, trust will be gradually eroded. It is difficult to build strong families, institutions, and communities on such a shaky relational foundation. This is why I think developing leaders who are firmly rooted in and committed to unwavering personal values and character traits is critical. I've said that if I am swayed by any voice in my ear, waiting for me to bend to their expectations, everyone will be watching who is in my ear. I do not mean that you should not listen to others and receive input. Rather, leaders should not be easily influenced by those who maintain poor or selfish motives.

As you think about who to develop as a leader, be sure to revisit your own core values, as well as those of your organization. Make sure you can use them as a litmus test for your own life, work, words, and actions. Then understand what you expect from others with respect to those values as you consider the kind of character you seek for the role of leader. Personally, I have drawn my values and intend for my character to reflect principles present in the Bible—principles that include loving God and loving others and being a servant and meeting others' needs. Additionally, the following are values that inform my life, and they also serve as the values of our organization. The descriptions of each value are action statements so that the value is not only an idea but also shows how and why we live it.

Passion

Passion is my first core value. Everything I choose to do, I do with passion. I commit my whole self to that purpose, aim, or task. At our company, "We drive with passion in everything because passion connects people to purpose." This book represents a current passion.

Passion is focused intensity on things that are of importance or great interest. Some have told me when they meet me that my level of intensity is a bit overwhelming. But it is who I am, and I am transparent about that. When my typical level of enthusiasm and intensity is not as apparent during an event or project, people who know me well tend to notice and ask about it.

Honesty and Integrity

Honesty and integrity, together, are the next elements that I use to define my character and that I tend to look for in leaders. These are paired because the root of integrity is honesty. Without it, integrity—the extent to which people feel that they can rely on what you say and know that you adhere unwaveringly to the values you proclaim—is threatened. I think of honesty as telling and accepting the truth, even when that truth is uncomfortable for myself or others. Integrity is abiding by and following through on those things that I've said I will do. At our company, "We live in honesty and integrity because without it our company and brand are hollow."

I will always voluntarily and freely tell the truth. I take my commitment to honesty and integrity so seriously that early on in our marriage, my wife and I had different perspectives on Santa Claus and the extent to which Santa would have a place in our Christmas traditions with our family. It didn't feel right to me to say or even imply that Santa was a real person who brought them gifts each year. I advocated for avoiding this tradition. She wanted the joy and fun of the experience for the kids. We decided that I would not voluntarily suggest that Santa isn't real, and if the kids asked, I would reply, "That's a great question for your mom!" They rarely asked any questions, it turns out.

I made the decision because I did not want to confuse my kids, and I didn't want there to be any reason at all to question whether I was telling the truth. If I was lying for fun, I reasoned, then it might be hard to discern between things that merit masking the truth or overtly lying "just for fun" and what things require clear and immediate truth telling in the years to come. Per my commitment to my wife, I never engaged in conversations about the role of Santa Claus in celebrating Christmas, and instead, she steered that for our family. I am intentional about reflecting on my honesty and integrity, even as it pertains to relatively simple or small scenarios. If I maintain a high standard, even in these relatively small and simple areas of my life, there will never be a need to introduce or entertain a different standard for any area or level of service and leadership.

Relationships

The third core value is relationships. This is evidenced through professionalism and by demonstrating respect for people, even if we disagree. I'll admit, this is not always easy for me, since there are always many different personalities and perspectives present in a large organization. It is sometimes difficult when there are those who disapprove of my perspectives, priorities, or decisions. As a leader, you will encounter this as well, and the leaders you develop should be prepared for this to happen during their journey. It is important to presume the best intent of others and productively process anger and frustration when conflict arises to maintain professionalism and be respectful amid it. At our company, "We build relationships because healthy success can only be created with mutual respect for others."

Again, Jesus modeled building relationships, even when costly. He was insulted, betrayed, tortured, and killed at the behest of the religious elite and at the hands of the Romans. His friends did not defend him. Upon His resurrection, He returned to bring assurance of His hope and commissioned the apostles to spread the Gospel and minister to others in the power of His Spirit. Jesus did not harbor ill will or express revenge toward those who had wronged Him. He never lost sight of

His purpose or the importance of relationships in the Kingdom. This is the way I want to live. No matter what has happened in the past, I will remain focused on my purpose, my passion, and on the future, building relationships with positive intent.

Serving

My fourth core value is serving other people. While the world often encourages centering oneself and self-service, this disposition will make it difficult to have a heart for serving others. At our company, "We serve our communities without hesitation."

Those who serve are motivated to prioritize others rather than themselves. Some revered leaders established their following by having a genuine focus on serving those they lead. Jesus modeled this powerfully, when He washed the feet of the disciples.[3] He inspired devotion and followship via His relatable teaching and compassionate service of others. He drew crowds of people and associated with those who were disliked, marginalized, and oppressed.

Learning

My final stated core value is learning. Learning requires understanding that you always have something else to discover and know. It takes humility. Much of my time outside of work or with my family is spent learning. I enjoy learning across an array of topics and interests. Whether I am studying sports, watching people, catching up on the latest cultural and political happenings, reading recent book releases, or consuming other written information, you will find me learning. Since I'm passionate about learning, most years, I read about one hundred books, and often consume dozens of pages of content per day.

Character

I choose specific topics, depending on what special projects I have. I tend to focus on books that inform my top priorities of faith, family, and productivity (work). I'm indebted to the many authors and leaders who have shared their ideas and experiences over the years. At work, we commit to "learn something every day by holding an open-minded approach to everything we do."

Learning is so critical because, of course, we're all works in progress. I don't want to have only my own singular voice, thoughts, and perspectives speaking into my life because, it turns out, that voice is sometimes wrong! When I read hundreds of authors and hear from countless commentators, I am processing the voices, insight, wisdom, and even a little ignorance thrown in based on myriad diverse insights and experiences. Personally, I still think our best ideas are disseminated through books. Yes, I know there's so many other good ways now to distribute content and ideas, but I really admire the ways that authors spend so much time and thoughtfulness crafting books. I've had a lot to learn about that process! When the book is published, authors are held accountable to the immortalized content. So, personally, my preference is to read books, since it makes it easier for me to reflect.

While I've shared my personal core values to illustrate some that you might consider in your own leadership journey, and as you identify other leaders to develop, I challenge you to think about the unique, defining characteristics of your character. Who are you when no one is looking? Does that align with who you say you are—your stated values? I encourage you to clearly describe these values and character traits and decide that they are immovable.

Then, as you identify leaders to develop, listen to who they say they are. Observe the extent to which they consistently live by those standards. Their ability to articulate and consistently demonstrate their core values illuminates their character. These values and their character are the foundation for the impact that they will have as a leader, so ensure that foundation is solid and reliable. If they have not defined their core values and cannot describe the character they hope to portray, or worse, do not stand by their stated ideals, I suggest that you might need to identify another person to develop, as they might not be ready for the role. Next, let's consider the role of charisma in potential leaders for you to develop.

CHAPTER 6

Charisma

Charisma is yet another factor to look out for when you are thinking about who to develop as a leader. While there is some argument around what charisma is exactly and how it supports effective leadership, nonetheless, people often associate charisma with leadership, and it is important not to overlook it. The public tends to embrace icons in sports, politics, or media who are highly charismatic. Let's think about what it is, why it matters, and how to spot it in others.

Influence and Energy

Charisma is a quality associated with the capacity to keep others' attention. Highly charismatic people have a physical presence and charm that invites and draws people to themselves and/or their ideas. Charismatic people have a magnetic effect. Everyone seems to be aware of where they are and what they are doing. They have an infectious energy, and people within their sphere want to share in that energy. People look forward to spending time with them, and they're missed when they're away. They have influence, since their words have more power to sway than others who might even be saying the same thing at the same time.

Martin Luther King Jr. was such a charismatic and inspirational leader. He had a great capacity, even early in his life, to communicate and influence. People listened to him speak on a litany of topics, and he could connect with many. He emboldened a movement, giving voice to Black people and bringing attention to oppressive and unjust systems that robbed marginalized groups of their civil and human rights.

Influencing Positively

Charisma is certainly not the only critical characteristic of effective leaders, and, of course, it is not unique to leaders necessarily. Many of our heroes on stage and screen have tremendous charisma, for example, but do not necessarily aspire to lead in other domains. So, as you consider the extent to which someone you might develop as a leader has charisma, ensure they transfer positive energy for others. A good way to determine whether their charisma is having a positive influence on others is to observe the verbal and nonverbal feedback of those they speak with. Don't watch the person; watch those who are watching them. It is possible to see the energy and positivity building. You can see them increase eye contact, nodding their heads, smiling, or moving away from conversations with others to draw nearer to hear and listen more intently. Someone with charisma might have a strong and noticeable voice that naturally commands and keeps others' attention. I have a friend and colleague who works for my company and has served as the master of ceremonies at our company's events. He's also the host of our podcast and serves in his local church reading Scripture for the worship team. His voice tone and presence cause people to sit up and listen. He can engender trust in contexts where it is helpful to have someone steering a large audience, to keep a group focused, bring clarity, and to reduce confusion. A potential leader who possesses charisma should be willing to share their platform with someone else and will always leverage their platform for good.

I always like to sit in the back of rooms. I started this purposeful habit in high school. While some people do this to be able to exit easily or avoid being distracting if they are on their phones or otherwise not paying attention, I do it to be able to observe the speaker and the listeners, to help inform and improve my own ability to speak and lead. I study the body language of the crowd and note whether they are watching the speaker or turning their heads and whispering. I look to see if the crowd is engaged, shifting in their seats uncomfortably, or looking at their phones. These are signs that can help determine if the speaker has lost their audience, and they might be an indicator of the extent to which the speaker possesses charisma. They may be the foremost thinker or expert on a topic and yet not be gifted at communicating and connecting their perspectives with the audience. If they lack charisma, they may be a valuable member of a team, contributing critical expertise and skills, but it might be challenging to lead when it is necessary to influence people to move or act. Importantly, there are other talents and methods to influence, for sure! Charisma can be helpful if it accompanies other capacities.

I remember a physics teacher in high school who made students want to come to class. They talked about his class in the hallways, and as they left, they had a pep in their step and a ton of energy. Students arrived early, stayed late, and turned their homework in on time. They were willing to do whatever he requested. He had a lot of charisma, and the students listened and followed his lead. Other educators had the same material, but many did not get the same engagement from students. This teacher infused palpable energy in the classroom. He understood timing, the power of a well-placed pause, and he could garner intrigue and demonstrate empathy. This all enriched his charm and endeared him to students. He had so much charisma and positively influenced the learning experiences of students.

I remember once seeing this teacher outside of school at a department store. He walked with the same energy and talked to the attendants. His charisma was evident in that completely different context as well. It was truly part of who he was. He loved physics, and he influenced the school environment beyond his classroom, including the department and school at large. His charismatic personality permeated every part of his life. Students were not the only ones who wanted to be in his presence. Teachers, administrators, parents, and others in the community did too.

People who have natural charisma display it everywhere they go—in a coffee shop, retail store, or on an airplane. It shows up in chance conversations and formal meeting places. They transfer positive energy as they share information, make a pitch, or tell a story. Their message and presentation tend to connect with their audience, irrespective of who that audience is. They aim to be someone worth listening to.

Transformative Communication

I began working on communication in college. It was my major. It's possible some people at the time would have said I have some natural charisma, and I expect just as many might disagree with that! In college, whenever I commanded the attention of others, I leveraged it for entertainment's sake. I learned that word choice, body language, vocal inflection, intonation, and many other speaking techniques affect the way an audience hears messages, as well as what they take away and remember.

In my first book, *Transform through Purpose: Your Path to Living an Authentic and Intentional Life*, I describe in some detail four different kinds of communication dynamics involved in sharing content. As you identify potential leaders to develop and consider the extent to which they are able to engage in charismatic communications, these might be helpful to you. The four kinds of communication include things we want people to know about us; things we think others want to know, generally; what we know the audience needs to hear or learn; and finally, information that will help the audience leave transformed. Ideally, people leave encounters with leaders feeling transformed.

Deeper, meaningful communication can inspire transformative outcomes when done thoughtfully and well. Charismatic leaders are often able to achieve this kind of communication. Transformational conversations result in positive changes in our mindset, as well as our behavior. These communication moments forever change people in a memorable way, sometimes on a small scale and sometimes significantly. These are pivotal moments in which one can gauge what life was like before and after that interaction. While sometimes those types of communications occur by happenstance, they can be intentionally planned, and as you identify leaders to develop, think about their ability to engage in communication that is transformative.

Early in my business career, I heard a speaker whose message was transformative for me. He described a significant personal and professional setback that he had. It was a mistake that threatened his career and cost the business a lot of money. He reflected on the event by saying he had a choice to be defined by what he had done or to be defined by what he did next. This perspective had an indelible impact on me.

He explained that he made choices pertaining to his attitude and subsequent actions. He could make excuses for his missteps, complain about the fallout, and place blame elsewhere. Or he could look for the lessons learned and decide how to conduct himself differently in the future to avoid such a mistake again. He described the temptation to dwell on the failure and its impact on his life and remain stuck and feeling hopeless and depressed. But he was determined to look ahead to the next opportunity, with more resolve. The speaker was charismatic, and his message was transformative. He had honed his communication skills and was focused and eager to help his audience learn and grow.

Charisma, when accompanied by other leadership qualities, can be a helpful indicator of potential as you consider who to invest in and develop. They may have potential to grow and develop as communicators and will ideally aspire to be transformative in their interactions. Intentional charismatic leaders can hone their talent and capacity to connect with others (as we will see in a forthcoming chapter) and help foster success for themselves and others. Regrettably, there are many examples throughout history where charisma was leveraged poorly by ill-motivated people, and it can be difficult to pin down exactly what is bound up in charisma. But when leveraged for good, it can be an incredible boost in helping teams to rally around shared outcomes.[1]

CHAPTER 7

Committed

The next characteristic to consider as you think about who to develop as a leader is whether they are committed. Nothing of value is created quickly. It takes months, years, and even decades to build something that makes a positive difference. However, the willingness of people to commit to anything today feels tenuous at best. It is common, for example, for people to jump from job to job or even to change career tracks, with the median tenure for employees hovering around four or five years.[1] Every year, thousands of college athletes enter the NCAA transfer portal looking for a different and better place to train and compete, and while for many that new opportunity is truly the best thing for everyone, many end up competing for multiple institutions throughout their career.[2] In many spaces today, it can be difficult to find people who are committed to a team, project, cause, or an organization.

Power in Perseverance

It is critical to identify leaders who have demonstrated commitment. Commitment is required to persevere through the ups and downs. Commitment enables leaders to learn and apply lessons along the way, cross the finish line of a plan or project, achieve objectives and celebrate accomplishments, and then set new goals that propel people and the organization forward.

It can be transformative to listen to sports champions, Hall of Famers, and MVPs talk about their journey to greatness. I've heard countless speeches by people who have reached the pinnacle of their respective fields, and not one of them says, "I am here because I was the first to quit when things got tough!" To belabor the point, I've never heard winners say, "My coach and fans appreciate me because they know that if the game is on the line, I consistently ask to come out of the game, rather than fight for the win. I'm prepared to exit the game a quitter." It's ridiculous to even imagine such a scenario because it is obvious that the one who wins does not quit. The victor likely never quit in key moments along the way. Champions refuse to throw in the towel, and they always find another way to win, even if an obstacle or challenge arises. I enjoy using such sports illustrations in talks and presentations because it's funny to even suggest that highly accomplished champions would demonstrate anything other than a mindset of commitment and perseverance.

In truth, no one can force an outcome or a result by effort alone. You may indeed fail a thousand times before seeing any gains, or you might experience immediate success. It can be difficult to predict, since there are usually many factors that are completely outside of your control. However, you can control the application of your energy. You can commit yourself to apply that energy throughout the ups and downs, the successes and the failures. I believe that, in the end, you will be defined more by your commitment than by the outcome. If you embrace that simple truth—that your committed effort defines you more than the result—it is even more motivating and fulfilling to spend your finite time and energy. Develop leaders who show this kind of internal motivation and commitment.

As you lead and develop other leaders, there will be tough days ahead. Do not invest your time in someone with a track record of quitting. Find leaders who commit with their whole mind, body, and soul! Such commitment may yield amazing results, but even if they fall short, the individual's character and leadership will be defined and refined in the process.

I'm personally inspired by the story of Ernest Shackleton, who led an expedition from London with the intent to traverse the little-explored continent of Antarctica. The team set sail on the ship *Endurance*, but the journey was thwarted when, in the early 1900s, it became trapped in ice in the Weddell Sea. After many months of drifting with the ice pack, the crew abandoned the ship and took precarious refuge on Elephant Island. The ship eventually sank to the bottom of the sea. Shackleton; Frank Worsley, the ship's captain; and a few other courageous crew members left their shipmates to undertake a journey in search of help. They sailed more than eight hundred miles over treacherous seas to South Georgia in a whaleboat. It took many weeks to find help and rescue the trapped crew. Shackleton believed that they would live, return to England, and see their families again. The team endured many trials throughout their journey, including frostbite, starvation, and terrifying weather events. He exerted strong will in the face of unusual trials, and his amazing feat showed the power of extreme hope and perseverance in the face of seemingly insurmountable odds.[3]

As the leader, Shackleton avoided negative thoughts and sacrificed his apportion of rations, sleep, and other comforts, determined to save his crew. He was fully committed to their survival, and remarkably, not one member of the crew of the *Endurance* died. The failed mission produced an inspiring account of a committed leader who was determined to save every last one of his men.

In our business, I've observed that the commitment of the owner is really a strong indicator of franchise success. When an owner is highly committed to the process and outcomes they want to achieve, they have far more likelihood of success. One franchise was in business for about ten years, and they had done well. I had a conversation with the owner, as they had decided they wanted to sell the franchise to one of their employees. As we discussed the reasons and the decision, the owner ultimately decided not to sell. Instead, they became determined to recommit to the company, the brand, and to learn how they could grow it even more in the future. Within just a few years of that conversation, the franchise saw tremendous improvement and experienced tremendous growth. Their leadership capacity escalated, and they earned Franchise of the Year recognition. Their recommitment to growth for themselves and their business was the key to seeing even more success. They became determined not to avoid the inevitable challenges and difficulties that come with running a business and instead decided to confront and proactively manage them so that the business did not get stuck. It is a success story for a committed leader.

As you decide which leaders to develop, consider their level of commitment to big *and* small things. Are they the first to quit, or do they endure? Do they consistently use the words "I can't" or "I won't"? Or do they find reasons that they can draw upon in the event of failure, even before a program, project, or initiative begins? These may be indications that they will quit and are not committed.

Focused on Others

Some people may be committed to a personally beneficial outcome, but they do not prioritize the development of the next generation of leaders. Look for those who have chosen to advance others ahead of themselves. They are not primarily motivated by the salary, a job title, or the next promotion. Instead, they want to help others lead well. They are intent on helping their community, family, or organization endure and grow for the good of others well into the future.

Marie Curie, the first woman to be awarded a Nobel Prize, emulated such commitment. She relentlessly pursued her research into radioactivity—a technology that is now indispensable for health-care providers who leverage this technology to diagnose and treat all manner of skeletal maladies. Her commitment to discovery was self-sacrificial, as she likely died of complications from repeated exposure to radiation at the age of sixty-six. Her work paved the way for development of noninvasive medical imaging techniques and informed a broad array of innovations in other scientific and medical applications.[4]

I imagine as you read about characteristics to look for in the people you want to develop as leaders, you're engaging in some self-reflection. Pause and ask yourself what you are most committed to. It is not possible to commit to many different things, so you must decide. Then, stick with it, regardless of the current and potential distractions. Model the commitment you want to see in the leaders you choose to develop. You cannot develop other committed leaders if you, yourself, do not demonstrate it by your words and actions. Look for those rare individuals with a special level of commitment to serving others and working for their benefit. This will help you develop a strong cadre of people to lead your organization far into the future.

CHAPTER 8

Collaborative

In nearly every circumstance and context, strong leaders must collaborate with others. Complicated, and even relatively simple, business problems require different talent, knowledge, and expertise to manage and solve. Leaders skillfully leverage team members' needs and capacities to navigate a path forward. Leaders are innately collaborative.

I've heard people say, "I try to collaborate, but others won't collaborate with me." What they often mean is, *I gave someone the information I thought that they needed. I told them what they should do, and then they didn't do it.* I've been guilty of this at times! This, of course, is not collaboration. Collaborative leaders commit to a jointly designed program or solution with shared responsibility for executing the program or solution.

Leading with Others

The United States military complex has historically leaned on a command-and-control style of leadership, with collaborative decision-making being, perhaps, less common. In this environment, orders come from the top, and they are not questioned. Subordinates are expected to execute on the orders they receive. The model likely was and is useful in some circumstances; however, other styles of leadership can be more effective. That said, there is some indication leadership styles are even evolving in the military to help solve complex problems. One Department of Defense article notes that military modernization involves cross-sector collaboration.[1]

Importantly, collaboration is undermined when people are focused on who gets the credit. The worst collaborators are generally those who are most eager to receive credit for a positive outcome. Strong collaborators feel energetic and excited about tackling new projects and focus on the jointly achieved outcome. They understand that a team can be much stronger together than the sum of its parts. Team members are free to use their diverse talents and skills more intentionally than they might otherwise be able to in a command-and-control environment, where people are assigned work but have little input on how they might best contribute to the work.

As you begin to identify leaders you want to develop, listen to their language and observe their actions. Collaborative leaders highlight others' contributions to the outcome and results. They are not focused on their personal accolades, nor the specific tasks they accomplished individually. They focus on the benefits of the collaborative effort and the long-term gains and the goals that the team advanced together.

I once had a project that required someone to lead. We needed to provide new uniforms for security officers. I looked for someone to fill a position responsible for coordinating the orders. When it came down to it, I had two solid candidates—each with different skill sets. During the interview process, I thought they could be strong collaborators, bringing different talents, knowledge, and skills to the company. So, I hired them both. For the first few months, they worked to figure out their roles and responsibilities, and months later, they exceeded expectations. They demonstrated humility and professionalism, working hard to learn each other's mindset and acknowledging the value the other brings to the team. They have since had some growth in their team and others appreciate working with them.

Collaborative efforts can yield outcomes that are more powerful than what individuals might accomplish alone. I'm fascinated by the way this is illustrated with animals that are yoked together. Their combined capacity to pull a load is greater than their individual capacity. The yoke helps the animals pull more efficiently, as the burden is balanced and shared. This is particularly true for Clydesdale horses, which are incredibly powerful animals with the ability to pull between two thousand and eight thousand pounds each. But when they are trained with another horse, their capacity can increase as much as fourfold!

Sharing the Lead and the Load

Humans could take a lot of cues from the animal kingdom when it comes to collaboration. I am from Nebraska. Our state boasts vast open landscapes and river systems that have attracted migrating birds for thousands of years via the Central Flyway. Sandhill cranes follow a fall and spring migration pattern, with a jaw-dropping hundreds of thousands of birds stopping over along the Platte River Basin and its tributaries every year. Like other species that travel thousands of miles during migration, they typically fly in a *V* formation, with a lead bird cutting through the air and wind, making the way easier and more efficient for the group. The lead bird will rotate along the way so that the energy and effort are distributed, maximizing the chances for the group to reach their destination intact and healthy. Sandhill cranes are adept at finding and catching thermal updrafts to aid their flight, and they communicate using loud calls to keep the group together along the path of least resistance. The birds work together, and the leaders do not get a plaque or certificate once they reach their destination. They don't update their résumé or create a social media post commemorating their success. Of course, the birds work naturally for the survival of the species, and their efforts are good for all.

This is not to say that celebration and recognition are not important. They are absolutely critical to a strong culture. But as it pertains to collaboration, leaders you choose to develop should find collaboration innately rewarding and encourage and model it.

I'd suggest choosing and developing leaders who collaborate well. Good collaboration results in outcomes that are collectively better than they would be for individuals working alone. Collaborative people direct credit and recognition to others, and they use resources around them wisely and remain focused on the process, as well as the desired outcomes. They recognize when it is time for another talented leader to take the lead. Like the lead bird in a *V* formation, leaders are always willing to do the hard work on behalf of and for the good of the process and the team. But they also recognize that others have much to contribute and can help prepare other leaders along the way. They know when it is time to let someone else take the lead. As you select who you want to invest in and develop, see that they're collaborators who value the gifts of others and can wisely include them in achieving outcomes.

CHAPTER 9

Connected

Connecting with others is yet another key characteristic to look for in leaders you hope to develop. When I was young, I struggled to find my social niche. While I liked learning things from lots of different people, I didn't fit in to any one group very well. I tended to think about what people in different groups needed from me. I tried to be my authentic self and connect with others as I could, being responsive to what I thought they might need. I tried to identify what we both liked and valued and figure out if there were small or big ways I could help. I looked for shared values rather than those things that were obviously different.

Leadership innately requires making connections—I'm glad I learned that early. The work of making connections never stagnates. Connections can be most easily made based on what is shared. Those connections can be used to steer, manage, and overcome differences.

Relational Bridge Building

The greater the number of connections, the greater the ability to connect quickly and meaningfully, which can multiply a leader's capacity to help and influence. Connecting involves many layers. Connected leaders tend to be empathetic. They understand others' emotions and what might underlie them. They tend to prioritize physical presence with people, but in our digital world, they may also have the ability to connect virtually, using technology and strong communication skills to bridge the gap. Connections can occur via networking with those they may not know yet or know well, and they may be able to facilitate friendships with many people. Again, I'm informed and encouraged by the fact that Jesus chose twelve disciples to be part of His closest circle. They chose to follow Him and were formed by His preaching and teaching. They listened and traveled with Him, and He had moments of connection with each of them.

Some people connect with others more easily. They might have the ability to know what others are thinking and feeling. You likely relate, as you think about a connection you have with someone who is like minded and you enjoy hanging out with. I'm always fascinated by studies of twins and the extent to which they know and feel what the other knows and feels. They seem to have a shared energy that heightens their commitment and relationship. While this is an unusual kind of connection and relationship that most of us cannot experience, it certainly is a unique model for what that kind of interpersonal connection could be like.

Again, seek those to develop who look for ways to connect with others. If there is a leader you want to develop, but you struggle to connect with them personally, it might be difficult to maintain a relationship with them. I would encourage you, however, to observe their capacity to connect with other people. It could be a great chance to build leadership in your organization when you find people with different abilities, insights, and capacities from your own. If you see that they connect well with many people—even if your own relationship seems to lack such a connection—maybe there is another person who can develop them. Don't miss out on the chance to elevate their leadership if the only hurdle seems to be your own personal relationship or connection. Rely on the evidence to decide whether they are a leader with the ability to grow!

People and Possibilities

Strong leaders are great at networking and building connections. Strong connectors aren't only good at being personable or comfortable in social situations; they see and anticipate the potential and the value of those connections in forwarding a cause or a purpose. They see possibilities in relationships and look for chances to offer help, service, advice, or support.

If you study people who can connect and network easily, you might notice they have a gift for filing away information and fun facts across a broad array of topics and may seem effortlessly conversational. Maybe they have and maintain relationships with many acquaintances and friends. They may make helpful introductions and have a superpower for remembering names or a fact or two about people and places, which they can draw upon in a moment's notice. They may remember faces well, or other aspects of the person and their preferences and interests or role. I like to use humor to make initial connections. I like to have fun! I find humor to be disarming, though I admit that not everyone may find my brand of humor entertaining.

Look for those who connect well and can expand their network. Determine if they are skillful at entering, contributing to, and even exiting conversations. Do they tend to ask good questions that provoke engaged responses? Do they practice strong listening skills and summarize what they heard well? Are they able to leverage the ability to connect with others with purposefulness that simply socializing well and being likable do not? Leaders with the capacity to connect enjoy moments of connection but also recognize the opportunities.

A connected leader enters a space and is naturally scanning for people they recognize. They might study body language and other details of the crowd. They see who is talking with whom, and they find a way to comfortably approach those they want to get to know and enter the conversation. They navigate different topics and look and listen to confirm interest and help center others in the conversation rather than themselves. Networkers find a way to have a follow-up conversation, sharing contact information or making plans to informally—or formally—meet again.

Follow-Up and Follow-Through

Strong connectors, who conduct meaningful networking, understand the criticality of follow-up. Initial introductions are valuable, but too many times someone offers the courtesy "Let's get together," which never actually happens. When a leader verbally makes that commitment but fails to follow through, their credibility is challenged. It is particularly awkward if you see that person again. The chance to create something positive from the initial encounter may be lost. Leaders understand that credibility is currency. Fulfilling commitments—even small ones—builds credibility. New connections are made and built upon a solid foundation of credibility. People want to expand their network to include leaders who are credible.

The leaders you choose to develop should be able to connect with others. They may be able to create a camaraderie and/or kinship that helps to build trust, which helps facilitate other work. They also need to be able to network effectively, which requires follow-through and maybe connecting others. They understand the power and potential of networking and leverage their memory of faces and names to have conversations and follow-up. Those who connect well help others feel like they have experienced a benefit from the interaction. They look forward to meeting that leader the next time. They are empathetic and can elevate others as they help them develop, building their leadership effectiveness.

As you identify and select leaders to develop, make sure they are people of strong character, who demonstrate follow-through and possess charisma that they use to influence others for good. Ensure that they are committed and collaborative, and, finally, consider whether your aspiring leader can connect and network purposefully. Few people embody each of these characteristics fully or completely, and, candidly, you might have other characteristics to add to this short list. But the future for many hangs in the balance of who you choose to lead, so select those individuals intentionally and wisely.

SECTION THREE

What Capacities Do Leaders Need?

I hope you now have more clarity about who you might develop as leaders. Next, you must think about what capacities your leaders should have to lead effectively. Importantly, you might mentor as part of your leadership development toolbox. Of course, mentoring and leadership development are not the same thing. A mentor may serve as a coach or guide, providing advice or direction for given circumstances. Mentoring is an excellent development tool for anyone, whether they aspire to lead or not. Developing leaders, though, is a long-term investment in the individual's future capacity to lead others to achieve individual and organizational purposes and goals.

In this section, we'll consider five key leadership capacities that can help prepare a leader for challenges and opportunities that they have not yet experienced, so that they are ready for them when the situation arises. Your future leaders will need to increase their level of understanding and mastery to leverage them in increasingly diverse and complex ways, depending upon their role and responsibility within your organization. They are intended to serve as a foundation for your leadership development framework and have broad application across organizations and include **visioning, strategic planning, financial acumen, team development, and project management.**

CHAPTER 10

Visioning

You'll first want your future leaders to develop the critical skill of visioning. In my experience, it is a skill most often neglected when developing leaders. If a leader does not have the ability to practice visioning, and thereby has no clear picture of what they want the organization to be and where they want it to go, then certainly it does not matter what you decide to do (strategic planning), the resources you have or require (financial acumen), who is coming along (team development), or what specific activities are required to get there (project management).

A Clear, Clarifying Picture

Visioning is the ability to see long term and to articulate an inspiring future state for the organization. Visioning includes acting as the catalyst for change that may be required to realize the shared vision.

While goal setting can be an important component of achieving a vision, it is not the same thing as creating one. A goal is a specific, often measurable and actionable objective that, ideally, if achieved, will bring an organization closer to realizing its future vision. A vision is a picture, and achieving goals helps to bring that picture into clearer focus. The vision is both informative and inspiring. You will want your future leaders to learn to create a vision that is concise and clear so that many inside—and outside—of the organization can understand it. Our company has a vision and goals for our franchises at each phase of their existence so that their growth is consistent and the company's strength and movement toward the future is assured.

Some leaders make the mistake of neither creating nor articulating a vision. They may set a goal, but in business, such goals tend to be responsive to the economy generally or the dynamics within a specific market. Goals are often set to please shareholders, employers, or customers, and they may be important to assess the state of the organization at a moment in time, but they are not the destination. However, leaders have often not stopped and reflected enough about where they want to take their organization, nor have they considered why they want to go there.

Understand the Past

In helping leaders learn to craft a vision, they should be encouraged to first study and understand the past. The context will help to inform what has been tried, what has been accomplished, and what has failed. They should identify what approaches or systems were effective and what things are replicable or which can be repurposed for the future. Help your leaders learn to ask reflective questions. What made one initiative work that is repeatable and sustainable? Sometimes things that are simple can have a profound and lasting effect on the long term.

Visioning

The wheel, as an all-too-obvious example, has been repurposed in all manner of inventions and advances in transportation for millennia. Technology has advanced exponentially since its invention, and yet, its fundamental utility is the same and has endured.

Think, too, about the rise of automobiles as a primary mode of transportation. The vision and plan for urban centers evolved accordingly. In the region of the original thirteen colonies, old roads resemble a plate of spaghetti. They generally followed the topography of the land, with construction following the path of least resistance, as they meandered from town to town. At the time those roads were established, in the seventeenth and eighteenth century, automobiles didn't exist. People traveled by horse or on foot. Today, if you go to Phoenix, Arizona, which dramatically expanded in the 1900s after cars came into popular use (and air conditioners, too!), you see the intentionality of the visionaries. They designed the city to make it easier to move around the city in automobiles. They wanted to support a fast-growing population that was always on the move. Now city planners are working on designing cities that best store and distribute energy and other resources to ensure their own sustainability as well as the environment's.

Scan the Current Environment

Again, help your leaders invite others to the task of scanning the current environment as they craft a vision. They will need to practice asking and listening to others who have ideas, research data and trends, and then spend time somewhere that inspires creativity to imagine what the best future can look like for the organization. Help them figure out what elements of the present state should be analyzed to inform the best possible future state of the organization.

Anticipate the Future

After reflecting on the past, and scanning the environment to understand the present state, help your leaders learn to anticipate the future. Some leaders prefer to put a time frame on their vision, looking five, or ten, or even twenty years ahead. As it pertains to our city planning illustration, I think the future vision for transportation includes expanded options for air travel. This vision has its challenges, for sure, but would eliminate challenges with road traffic, which is increasingly unsafe and requires constantly addressing maintenance and construction needs, which are costly. I'm not in this line of work, specifically, but city planning and transportation trends influence our organization, which uses automobiles for security patrolling, so it's important to continue looking to the future for how the work may change or could evolve.

Your future leaders must develop a capacity for visioning. They must know the tools they need to create that picture of the best possible future. They should learn to reflect on the past, scan the current environment for the relevant data and information, and, finally, craft a compelling vision for the future that includes elements that need to be preserved and an inspiring picture that realizes potential. When new to the leadership journey, your future leaders might start by crafting a vision for small parts of the organization, such as a project or a one-time event or initiative. If you are in a restaurant, a budding leader could be tasked with creating a future vision for seating and waiting on guests, or a new engineer with leadership potential might be tasked with crafting a vision for a new internship program. As a leader progresses in their journey, the vision they craft could have greater implication and influence over larger portions of the organization. Irrespective of the scope and complexity of the organization, the basic framework for visioning can be expanded and repeated. Your new leaders should understand the role that vision plays in moving people and the organization forward, then learn to craft and communicate in a way that is vivid, informed, and inspiring.

CHAPTER 11

Strategic Planning

In addition to visioning, your future leaders must develop their capacity to think and plan strategically. Strategic planning involves forming and prioritizing plans to attain long-term goals. It includes capitalizing on opportunities while managing challenges and risks. A strategic plan is a map to the future that ensures the organization will accomplish its vision.

Happy Customers

A strategic plan accounts for the recent past and the present circumstances and is informed by feedback from experts and other relevant data. It includes key focus areas and achievable goals that are measurable and aligned with the vision. Most organizations include various kinds of sales and revenue growth for their strategic planning goals, but it's important to note that growth happens as a downstream indicator of a well-formed and well-executed strategic plan.

In strategic planning, I tend to begin with the vision and then review the purpose of our company, which exists to create peace of mind. I keep a happy customer in mind, which happens when franchisees and their security teams are caring well for and anticipating their customers' needs. I think about specific kinds of customers and the environments they have and what they will need to inform specific elements of the strategic plan. With those customer lanes in mind, we build plans to clarify and quantify success and to build our brand awareness in the market. In short, the strategic plan creates a tangible and operational structure for the business over a defined period, say five or even ten years.

Reduce Confusion

Last year, our family experienced a lot of changes and moves. After twenty years in our home, we moved to a new one. Our oldest graduated from college and moved to a new city in a different state. Our third child graduated from high school and went away to college. This all happened within three months. As a family of six going in different directions, there was a vision for the future that drove each of these moves, and for them to happen without a hitch, there needed to be a clear plan. Whether you are moving your family or moving your organization forward through changes and opportunities, the strategic plan will determine the level of success you experience. The goals you set to achieve over a given period will require and encourage others to be a part of your plan. Everyone should see themselves somewhere in the strategic plan and how their work or responsibility is relevant to the plan.

Strategic Planning

Maybe, like me, you have been asked by a friend or family member to help them move. You might have a vision of how you would move yourself, and as you (maybe begrudgingly!) accept the responsibility to help your friend and commit your time and effort, you might expect there to be a plan of some kind. And if instead, you arrive at your friend's house to see that not a single thing has been packed, the only vehicle to move items is a small pickup, and there aren't even any boxes or tape to pack anything, it feels discouraging and compounds the exhaustion. This is a small example of the negative impact of having a vision without a strategic plan in place to help make it happen. On the other hand, when you arrive to help friends or family move and see that much work has already happened ahead of moving day, and there is a clear plan in place for loading, transporting, and unloading the items, it is motivating and encouraging. When the plan is clearly communicated to the moving crew, and food and beverages are provided, even though the work is still hard, it feels far more satisfying for everyone once the work is done. For an organization, it's, frankly, no different. The implications of not having a thoughtful strategic plan can be significant, leading to exhaustion with little view of why work matters and what people are working toward. However, the chance to accelerate success is multiplied when a strong strategic plan is adopted and shared and progress tracked.

Strategic plans can take time to build. Sometimes it could take weeks or months to carefully consider and analyze each of the relevant details. Inevitably, strategic plans require operational plans to be executed. Some people remain in strategic thinking mode, while others are more comfortable thinking operationally. Both are valuable for the process, but leaders should be able to recognize the differences. When a plan is perfectly designed, it can be more efficiently executed. Each person involved in operationalizing the plan can see the future and has clarity about what they are supposed to do. Effective leaders know how to carefully craft and communicate an effective strategic plan. They also connect the strategic plan to the big vision.

A Strategic Planning Framework

Help your future leaders learn to thoroughly review and reflect on purpose and vision to establish the foundation of the strategic plan. Creating a strategic plan that does not align with the vision can confuse teams and the organization overall. It is difficult to invite people to help establish a strategic plan that is unclear in how it promotes the vision of the organization. A plan aligned to the vision is inspiring and purposeful. Then, encourage your leaders to review the purpose and mission of your organization so that the strategic plan reflects what you say your organization does and why it does it.

Next, help your leaders determine the duration of and timing for the plan. It is imperative to think about how long it will take to accomplish the plan and what is realistic. Typical strategic plans for smaller organizations are three- or five-year plans. Many plan as much as ten years out. Initiating the plan is, of course, dependent upon talent and resources. Timing matters when developing strategic plans.

The final pillar in the strategic plan approach is to audit and assemble the requisite resources. Resources include money and talent. When I was growing up, I loved to watch the show *MacGyver*. Every episode, MacGyver found himself in some kind of trouble from which he had to escape. And, of course, there was always a suspenseful time crunch involved. His amazing skill was to look around the room and determine what resources he could repurpose to solve the dilemma. He developed a sequential plan quickly, and step-by-step, he executed on it.

Strategic Planning

Similarly, leaders build strategic plans and are cognizant of the urgency to accomplish their vision. They take advantage of the circumstances and timing to maximize resources and thereby improve their chances for success. Strategic plans include areas of focus and goals, but to have utility, they also need to include a step-by-step action plan that is clearly and regularly communicated, just like when you're relocating friends or family. Once the plan is developed, communicated, and set in motion, it is important to touch base regularly throughout the project management phase and ensure progress is made and to make necessary adjustments.

Help your leaders understand that effective leaders can not only craft a compelling vision for the future, but they're also able to think and plan strategically to help ensure that the organization can accomplish that vision. Help your future leaders learn that no vision comes to fruition without a thoughtfully constructed and diligently executed strategic plan. It is discouraging for employees or volunteers in an organization to adopt the excitement of the leader about the future vision only to realize later that they have no plan at all for achieving it and no clarity about who and what is needed to get there. But it can be fantastically engaging to share your skills, experiences, and expertise with an organization that has an inspiring vision and a strategic plan with milestones and assigned responsibilities for accomplishing it.

CHAPTER 12

Financial Acumen

In addition to vision crafting and strategic planning, leaders must develop a capacity for financial acumen. Again, this section serves as a framework to inform your leadership development approach and features an overview of principles I think are critical for helping leaders develop a capacity for financial acumen.

Multifaceted Financial Acumen

It is important to help your leaders develop a capacity for different aspects and elements of financial acumen. Financial acumen includes an understanding of the costs and pricing per unit and the value and cost of producing the product or providing the service at scale. It includes insights into customers' needs and propensity to buy. It requires properly positioning and distributing products and services in perfect alignment with those customers' needs, to maximize and take advantage of current and future trends.

This leadership capacity, in my experience, is the toughest for leaders to apply. I have met leaders who are amazing at managing their organization's financial numbers, for example. They know what their costs are. They know the total revenue they are generating by division, service, or product, and they know their margins. Often, however, they are very risk averse. They don't know when to invest money, nor do they know how to generate new ideas and innovate in ways that drive the business and expand their purpose or drive earnings. While they can analyze the current financial state and carefully track the organization's finances, they struggle with decision-making that is relevant to driving innovation and expansion.

On the other hand, there are organizational leaders who struggle to manage costs, budgets, and other financial considerations. They can't tell you costs or budgets, and they don't understand project scope and pricing. They may understand the core value proposition of the product or service they offer, and they may understand their customers' needs and where to market their products and services. They might even have passion and commitment that results in some results and returns. However, without a sound, grounded understanding of their profits and losses and other financial data, they will have a difficult time making decisions that drive expansion and growth.

Leave Room for Doing Good

As you develop future leaders, they must develop their financial acumen. This includes not only managing and stewarding money and resources and analyzing spreadsheets and growing profit margins but also ensuring that you do no harm and practice generosity in the process. Leaders should be trained and encouraged to leverage success and create financially viable and thriving organizations for the good of the organization, people, and communities.

Some may not think of Jesus as a beacon of financial acumen, but along my own faith journey, I've learned important financial lessons concerning management of money and finances from His life and ministry. He admonished those who hoarded resources only for their own gain, and He preached that people should "give to those who ask, and don't turn away from those who want to borrow."[1] His parables, such as that of the prodigal son, steered His hearers and disciples to be generous and forgiving, but also to be unselfish in their pursuit of a good life for themselves and others.[2] His stories reveal the harm that often results when care for others is disregarded and there is no generous stewardship. Jesus emphasized sacrificial giving, praising the widow who gave a small amount to the temple treasury. Her gift was more valued and meaningful than the offerings of the wealthy who contributed out of their abundance—the widow's humble gift was most noticeable to God.[3] He admonished the love of money, which distracts from the kind of practices that are honoring to God.

Jesus warned against habits and spending on things that did not have eternal value, warning his followers not to "store up treasures here on earth, where moths eat them and rust destroys them, and where thieves break in and steal."[4] He was always attentive to the ill and the poor, seeing and meeting their needs, while condemning those in leadership who oppressed them for their own gain.[5] He was intent on developing and growing people to serve and lead for the benefit of others rather than at others' expense.

I've always aimed to tip generously. I have particular care for moms and moms-to-be who work in the service industry. I tip food servers, baristas, and hairdressers well when I receive good service, occasionally even more than the cost of the service provided. I believe that being too attentive to the percentages or the total dollar tipped can result in missing a great opportunity to encourage or help someone who might need support during a hardship or transition. A miserly mindset that is immovable and fixed keeps you from enjoying chances to help others financially in life and in business. Aspiring leaders should be wary of adopting such a mindset, which will result in missing out on the joy inherent in being generous.

Beware of Financial Curmudgeons

I once had a very miserly coworker. He was always trying to find the best deal. Decades ago, when digital cameras were first coming out, we traveled together to China. There was an assumption that digital cameras would be cheaper there. My colleague wanted to buy one to bring back home. The salesperson realized that he was a miserly buyer and would not pay the market price for the camera. After a full hour of discussion, the shop owner suggested that he get a camera with more pixels and memory, and he would even offer it to him for less than he was willing to pay. My colleague agreed. The shop owner said if my coworker was willing to purchase two cameras, he would discount them another 5 percent. The coworker bought two cameras, with the intent to sell the other back home to help boost his earnings and ensure he received the best possible deal. The shop owner ran his credit card, and he took the camera out of the store. When we returned to the hotel, he looked up the price of the camera back home. He realized that he had overpaid for that brand of camera by about 20 percent over what the camera retailed for in the United States! Sometimes being miserly and having a myopic focus on the dollars and cents means losing sight of the actual value you hope to gain when exchanging money for goods or services. Make sure your future leaders do not fall into the trap of inordinately focusing on minutiae, which can result in missing bigger-picture opportunities.

If the extent of financial acumen includes only careful attention to certain cells on the balance sheet, your leaders might need to shift focus to include assessing and understanding the real, long-term value of the product or service. Value refers not only to the cost of something but also reflects the durability and potential returns the product or service will create in the long run.

Dollars and Cents Do Matter

Financial acumen means having a grasp on drivers of organizational revenue and growth, profitability and cash flow, and the impact of business decisions on value creation for your product or service, among other things. Financial acumen includes thoroughly understanding the costs involved in producing and bringing the product or service to market, as well as the market's perception of that value and willingness to pay. Plenty of resources and training exist for business finance, and, of course, it's not my intent to include many technical pieces in this book; however, as you look for leaders to develop, especially at higher levels of your organization, the need for this capacity grows, and their financial sophistication must grow with it.

Again, some business leaders and entrepreneurs understand the value, need, or current demand for their product in the marketplace but struggle to understand production, labor, or other costs required to market the product or service broadly. This is often highlighted on *Shark Tank*. If an entrepreneur steps onto the *Shark Tank* stage, they must know their financial numbers to secure an investment from one of the sharks. Most entrepreneurs on the show seem to understand their product or service, their current and potential market, the demand, and even potential price points that might make that product or service a viable commodity. Most seem to demonstrate and/or describe their product with energy and enthusiasm without missing a beat in their initial pitch. However, as the discussion progresses, the sharks start asking about the numbers—the finances—for the company. It is not uncommon to see leaders who lack business finance acumen lose momentum and energy and stumble with their responses. Confidence and passion visibly and audibly dip and wane. After a handful of questions, if an entrepreneur has unclear answers, with no convincing, scalable understanding of the numbers, they don't get an offer of investment in their business, or they are unable to respond to the one that they receive in a productive way. The entrepreneurs walk away disheartened. Some immediately begin to regenerate their enthusiasm for their idea and product but are unsure about resourcing needed to help scale the business.

Naturally, investors are less passionate than the entrepreneur/innovator about the product or service. Their intent is to invest in a business that will result in a return. The passion of the leader could be skewing their vision of the economics of the situation, or perhaps they simply don't possess the skills and knowledge needed to make the financial plan. The result is, again, a missed opportunity to grow. A leader who is miserly is blinded by the details of the dollars and cents to the extent that they are unable to assess potential opportunities. A passionate leader who is blinded by their excitement for their idea or innovation but incapable of understanding the P&L will likely be unable to maximize their potential opportunities.

Don't Get Stuck

Whether you have a leader who tends to be miserly, always beholden to the spreadsheet, or a leader who is full of passion but unable to assess and project financial needs and possibilities, they risk getting stuck as they try to map a path forward. And getting stuck not only has implications for the leader but also for those who are influenced by the leader. Therefore, it is imperative to strike that balance, to demonstrate financial acumen that brings growth and realizes possibilities—that balances strong awareness of finances with passion for the product and its viability in the market.

Again, financial acumen balances the core economics associated with bringing a product or service to market with savviness around the benefits of that product or service by clearly representing the problems it solves for individuals within the core market. Understanding value starts first with the cost of the problem that the product or service is trying to solve. In other words, what is the cost of *not* fixing the problem. Value also includes understanding the money that is needed for investment, as well as the durability of the product or service.

Leaders need to be able to make financial decisions—sometimes quickly—that account for the best value and potential returns in the long term. It can be difficult to make financial decisions in the moment. Leaders are susceptible to feeling trapped by budgets and line items on the spreadsheet or, on the other extreme, driven by passion and excitement to take a product to market. The key for leaders is to weigh the value and opportunity in the long term. Understand and note financial implications, consider the opportunity to resolve an identified problem or opportunity, and make the decision that will bring the most value to the most people over the longest period of time. Future leaders should review recent decisions that they have made and analyze what data and processes they typically use to make those decisions. Help your leaders reflect on whether they land on decisions that result in bringing financial and experiential value, tend to be unsound financially, or are stuck in short-sighted decision-making driven by numbers and spreadsheets.

Returns Are the Thing

Businesses sometimes make the mistake of going big on marketing and advertising for some misguided reasons. Passionate business owners, for example, may try to reach the masses by investing in a Super Bowl ad. They might reason that millions of people will see it, and they only need 1 percent of viewers (let's say that number is 500,000) to buy to recover the advertising investment back. Then the business will have a ton of brand exposure!

On the other hand, highly budget-conscious leaders might not invest in marketing at all due to the high price point and the subsequent risk to the financial solvency of the organization of such a large expenditure that may or may not have a return. Passionate people might reason that all they need to do is get a strong distribution of the product that will result in selling the product and seeing a return. In any case, the goal is to ensure that the per-unit price of the product can be sold and distributed at high enough volume to recover the cost and expand the business footprint; for many, such a placement is a high-risk proposition with little lasting value.

Again, your leaders must consider how to get their product or service out and available. If there is no marketing, there's obviously little opportunity to build brand awareness, and the products will sit on the shelves. Of course, if you do not sell the product, the result is having no margin, because cost savings were the prevailing driver of the decision.

Leaders must understand the balance between the passion-led decisions of brand exposure and the cost-conscious decision of not spending the money, which drives costs. It depends on the return if it's worth it or not. It's not the size of the initial investment but the return that underlies the wisdom in the decision.

The Beachside Vendor

I once met a beachside vendor who understood this concept well. He had a kiosk cart that he had invested in and stocked with products. He was energetic and enthusiastic, unlike most of his peers, who had their things set out, leaving it to customers to decide what was best for them to buy. There was passivity in their method of selling. The vendor who impressed me studied the people and what they valued. He had a little bit of everything, knowing what customers needed and preferred. He had a singular price point: All items were ten dollars. He seemed to understand that the price was of less consequence to his market than the value of the products they bought from him. When he saw a couple walking by, he suggested that the gentleman purchase flowers for his significant other. If a balding person passed by, he would offer to sell a hat to protect their skin from the summer sun. If there was a family with kids, he sold them beach toys—all for ten dollars each. When there was rain in the forecast, of course, he had umbrellas. When it was hot, he had those same umbrellas ready to block the sun. His salesmanship was stellar, and he knew his margins for each item and for the business overall, and his goal was volume. He responded to needs and opportunities and capitalized upon each moment. He worked to benefit the customer, had an appropriate price point and margins, and drove sales volume to help build his revenue.

As you develop your leaders, help them keep that savvy beachside vendor in mind. Always consider what the circumstances dictate, and always know what decision and what sale will result in the most long-term value for the business and the customers. Sometimes that means your next steps will require a greater financial investment. Other times, you will need to pull back the investment you are making. In either case, leaders must understand the cost to bring the product or service to market. Leaders anticipate expected returns and, as stated, most of all, consider the enduring value that the product or service brings to the organization and the customer. Leverage these perspectives to grow your leaders' capacity for financial acumen, so they can move forward with the strategic plan and accomplish the vision.

CHAPTER 13

Team Development

Leaders must build their capacity to craft a vision, develop a strategic plan, and use financial acumen to make critical resourcing decisions. They must also have the capacity to develop teams.

Different Abilities, Shared Goals

Help your leaders learn to develop strong teams. Team development involves inspiring commitment, uplifting spirits, generating pride around the work, building trust, and engaging and motivating team members to excel. Team development means inviting individuals to rally around a shared goal, even though each might have different roles and responsibilities and contribute different strengths as they work to achieve that shared goal. A team is collectively more effective and successful when collaborating in concert rather than as individuals working in silos. Leaders typically understand that they need talented team members with skills to help their group or organization succeed. Sometimes teams are formed for short-term objectives, and sometimes a team is more permanent and works toward long-term goals.

It is refreshing to work on teams where each member is passionate about accomplishing a shared vision and is not only motivated by a title or paycheck. I have said that entitlement starts with the title. Occasionally, there are team members who are driven primarily by ego rather than the shared vision and purpose. They can create a political environment that pushes away others and creates organizational silos. These individuals may be so fixated on getting credit that they accomplish things at others' expense, and others sometimes don't want to work with them. You cannot build a team with those who have self-interest as their greatest driver. This is the purpose and importance of the vision and the plan—to inform the development of the right team.

A couple of years ago, I decided to begin pulling my ideas and experiences together in a way that I could share them. I first decided to start a podcast, as I mentioned in a previous chapter. I'd never done it before and knew that I needed a team to help make it happen. I recruited my friend and colleague to cohost, as I knew he had a perfect face for radio—our running bad joke! I recruited a partner with production expertise, a strategic content manager and producer to help steer and keep us on track, and someone with technical and marketing expertise to help us get the material recorded and distributed, among other contributors. We're still trying to figure out how to do it best, and we need each person's respective knowledge and skills to pull it off, but the project has really been a lot of fun. It's a simple example of how to be most productive at work: Build a team with shared vision. Ensure the desired outcomes are clear, and free team members to do what they do best.

Team Development

Keep the Capacities Rightly Ordered

Many times, I've heard leaders say, "If I had the right team in place, then I could accomplish so much!" They think that they have an idea, and the very next step is building the team. However, as described in the previous chapter, crafting a vision must come first. Effective teams have clarity about the vision and will rally around one that feels bigger than themselves. If you bring in a team that is disinterested in being part of a vision that transcends their current experience, it will be difficult to accomplish that vision.

If you only have a vision and no strategic plan to accomplish it, you cannot build a team; you will just gather fans! Fans have a level of commitment to a team or a program, but they are generally present to be entertained—to simply enjoy the show. When there is no strategic plan in place to steer how to operationalize a vision, you can end up with lots of well-meaning people standing around, observing the show with little to no clarity about how they can contribute to accomplishing the vision or achieving the strategic plan. This scenario is a recipe for burnout for leaders who then take on the responsibility of executing the plan without sharing the load with those who have talent and capacity to do the work best. They get exhausted as they expend energy trying to do the job of the whole team instead of developing one. Team development, at its core, is about building a highly motivated team where each team member knows exactly what they contribute, and they share a vision for what they are trying to accomplish that they couldn't accomplish on their own.

Even with a compelling vision, a workable strategic plan in place, and a talented team assembled, if the leader lacks savvy financial acumen, success is not likely to last long. We see this with big ideas that happened during the dot-com bubble of the mid- to late 1990s that eventually burst. There were big ideas of what tech could do for our lives. Some likely had a strategic plan for how they would get the business off the ground and some even had financing; however, there was never a viable return on the investment or a customer base that would sustain it. As a result, the show quickly ended, companies laid off people, and many closed their doors or were acquired with little to no return for their investors.

I'm a big fan of the movie *Field of Dreams*, where we get that famous quote "If you build it, they will come." Ray Kinsella, an Iowa farmer, receives a daring—even crazy—vision of building a baseball field in a field of corn. He crafts the plan and gets the resources together to build it. In the end, the team walks out from the cornfield onto the field. Cars line up to enter the field—eager to share in the dream becoming reality. It is a picture of reconciliation and hope for the future. Without the vision, plan, or capacity to influence the needed resources, the team would have had no context or opportunity to play.

I once had an opportunity to go to Panama and see the Panama Canal. If you have never been, I recommend you put it on your bucket list to go! It is one of my favorite man-made creations. As I watched videos on the Canal, studied how it operates, and saw the outcomes, I appreciated the vision, the strategic plan, the financial resourcing, and the team development that were required to make it all happen. The vision was to create quicker passage from the Atlantic to the Pacific Ocean to facilitate better, more efficient commerce and trade—a vision that had been around for centuries![1] The Canal would save many days—weeks, even—of travel time for ships, avoiding the need to round the tip of South America.

The plan included myriad land surveys across Central America to determine the best path for constructing the canal. There were other areas with less distance to cross for construction but which were less favorable for constructing the passage. During this process, they realized there was a large lake between the shores on the east and the west of the continent, and if they created dams to contain the water and subsequently flood the lake to create locks to help manage the water flow for the ships, they could leverage these locks and the lake to allow the boats to pass through.

The most fascinating part to me is that there were thousands of workers from over dozens of nations, speaking dozens of languages, fighting the challenges of the area, and within a matter of years, they had a functioning canal. The team had a goal and worked effectively, in no small part because the vision and the plan were clear. The feat is particularly incredible when you realize the incredible resources, human cost, and energy it required to build it—and at a time when the equipment and technology were less sophisticated than what is available today.[2]

Set the Trajectory

Help your leaders develop these capacities by initiating a trajectory rather than only checking off topics to review or completing seemingly disconnected tasks along the way. Point them in a direction, demonstrate a process, and coach them along the way.

The methodology of "I do, you watch; we do together; you do, I observe; you do on your own with me available to support and coach along the way" is a generally effective "process" for setting leaders on the leadership trajectory. If you have been a leader in any context for a while, you understand that it is impossible to train a new leader on every possible scenario. You share principles and frameworks so that they can apply them during each experience.

Now, let's break this down in an even more practical way. Any time we bring a new person to our organization, I meet with them to establish and ensure vision alignment of what our security franchise firm aims to do, which is to build a global, leading security brand. We discuss the strategic plan as it pertains to their role and then discuss the investments I am willing to make in them, their role, and their work. I ask them who they are and why they are here at our company. I ask what they want to do, so I can support them better. I have a responsibility to communicate the vision and consistently work to empower them to fulfill their work and role.

After this conversation, we discuss their next steps. Many times, I find they are fixated on performing well on the task to get my approval. I always tell them that, whether they excelled at that first task or not, I don't assign initial steps on the first day or week that would be particularly world changing for the organization, of course. I am not watching the outcome per se but instead watching the process they use to achieve the task. Essentially, I am working with them to calibrate their skills around a process and determine their approach to a different task. The hope is that they can accomplish it well, then refine and repeat the approach in a different scenario.

It is always most critical to me to see a leader's confidence rise as they work through a new problem or bring to life a new project. It's gratifying to see success in action and watch them enjoy those moments. They don't always happen right out of the gate, but those successes are always worth the continued practice and effort.

Improvement over Perfection

As you help leaders build their capacity to develop teams, make sure they first and foremost communicate the vision and expectations for the team. I lead with the expectation that the work will get better with every attempt and that the team will move closer toward the

Team Development

goal(s)—not that they will be perfect out of the gate. To develop the team, ensure that you focus on communicating ways team members can develop their skills in the moment. Good sports coaching is best done with video or in the moment that a skill is being executed. Additionally, research is clear about the value of recognition and praise at work, so be sure to acknowledge excellence and recognize team members' strengths and effort.

In addition to setting the expectation for improvement, the team will need to know a step-by-step process. Some have more difficulty thinking stepwise than others. Help leaders know to look for those who understand and can replicate and improve strong processes. Have leaders practice breaking down simpler tasks in a step-by-step way and progress to more complexity as they learn. It can be difficult to do this well for even relatively simple processes. As a fun training exercise, help them practice thinking through each step needed to respond to an email or set up a new client within your client management system. It brings self-awareness to leaders who are wanting to help teams understand processes that can be far more complex than these simple tasks. And steps that seem simple to people who have done them multiple times are often overlooked, and team members are then chastised for not getting it right, when no one pointed out the step! Be sure they learn how to share steps, so the team is set up for success. Then, as team members grow and practice, they can perform the work at a higher level—more efficiently and/or more effectively.

When a leader meets with their team, they identify each of the key areas they need to learn and focus on to be successful. As a people manager, I adopt repetitive processes, regardless of who I am managing. I define a task and outline the steps needed to excel at it. I then show them the process and challenge them to always improve performance in the steps. When I work with team members, they accelerate their own development, if they have strong self-awareness and reflection on their skills and performance. They do this best when they know what is expected of them, are encouraged and recognized for improving their performance, are more efficient, and in the end, begin to live an even better, more productive life in the organization! Our large intern programs are fundamentally about giving young professionals the chance to be part of a team and help them prepare to work in a professional environment. I give them projects, opportunities, and lots of chances to be successful. The most successful of them might move into other roles.

Team Development Starts with the Leader

I've realized, over my professional career, that a team's success hinges on the capacities of the leader. Help your leaders value and initiate self-development. You cannot own all their growth; help them own it for themselves. A hobby of mine is reflecting on the routine of my day to see what I can do to improve and make it more efficient. When I was in my twenties, it took me twenty-five to thirty minutes to get ready for work. I would wake up, shower, get dressed, eat breakfast, etc., and then head out to work. As I looked at the steps to get my day started, I realized the one that I could improve upon most was preparing and eating breakfast. I used to make eggs, drive to McDonald's, or grab different items to eat from the kitchen. I decided I didn't want to wait in traffic to go get something. I wanted to be in the kitchen with my kids before our day began, but I wanted to be efficient. I knew I needed to rehydrate in the morning and that I wanted eggs for protein and caffeine to jump-start the day. It generally took me about ten to fifteen minutes to get breakfast. I now have it down to about ninety seconds! I heat up precooked egg bites, which are in the dairy section of the grocery store and only require a few seconds to heat up in the microwave.

I grab a water bottle boosted with electrolytes and a premade bottle of cold coffee, and I consume them in the car on the way to work. I'm not too choosy, as you can see, about my menu items for breakfast, so this does the trick for me.

You may not be as maniacal about routine and your improvement tactics! But leaders, as a rule, need to be self-reflective and seek to develop themselves. The pinnacle of team development happens as the leaders practice self-development. Develop leaders who regularly look for ways they can get and be better. They may have more capacity to develop teams because they start by developing themselves.

Development Is Often Incremental

The difference that small changes and growth can make is encouraging. In my small example of making mornings more efficient, if I save just ten minutes in preparing and eating breakfast every morning, I could save as much as 3,600 minutes per year—sixty hours! This means I potentially free up an additional week and a half of time spent focused on my top priorities. These hours are typically spent having conversations with my wife and kids, heading to work a bit sooner, or increasing my morning productivity time before meetings. Little improvements in self-development and team development can truly have a huge impact.

To develop leaders who build sustainable, growing, and world-changing organizations, leaders need capacity for team development. Set clear expectations, focus on improvement, identify the step-by-step processes needed for success, establish goals and targets, ensure the leader is modeling self-development—then the team analyzes steps and details that will improve the process and the outcomes. Collaborative work between the leader and team can help make a vision become reality.

CHAPTER 14

Project Management

Building on the idea that process improvement matters in team development, project management is also an important capacity for leaders to develop. A well-conceptualized and well-managed project yields positive outcomes and strong momentum toward the strategic plan and the vision of an organization. Likewise, a poorly conceptualized and poorly managed project yields frustration and a sense of hopelessness that the objectives will ever be accomplished.

Project Management Mainstays

Project management is making decisions and analyzing problems to produce high-quality results that surpass customer expectations. This work can conjure up an array of emotions for leaders throughout the duration of a project. Unexpected and unanticipated delays, lack of clarity of roles, out of control egos, or team members who fail to follow through can all cause frustration and stymie progress.

Organizations can engage in many project types. Some are a regular part of operations, and other special projects may include one-off or periodic initiatives. Our annual convention has innumerable projects that are required to pull off an excellent experience for our franchisees, and I think it is one of our company's best project-management leadership success stories. For more than a decade, we've had an external partner to our organization who has led the project planning. She is extremely skilled in identifying the many areas of responsibility that are needed to host an excellent, multiday event. She partners with dozens of team members across the country within our own organization, navigates and negotiates needs with the host venue, and partners with other area organizations involved in the numerous on-site and off-site activities that are part of each year's program. She keeps the outcomes consistently in mind and is highly collaborative. Her leadership in this increasingly complex project—due to our growing company, and thereby growing numbers of attendees and activities—makes the project increasingly complex, and her capacity to lead it has grown with it. The result is a consistently excellent event that helps us shape and strengthen our company's culture over time.

Assuming a leadership role for a poorly conceptualized and poorly managed project might at first feel like a tremendous opportunity. However, leaders may come to realize that the resourcing, funding, and process in place never made sense in the first place. It could be that critical initial steps for the project were not well thought out or the project may not align with the goals outlined in the strategic plan. Sometimes teams will see a project through to the end only to realize it didn't serve the vision, and the outcomes were neither relevant nor useful. Help your leaders fight pressure or inertia to hop into a project before understanding the overarching vision, the plan, and the needed resources and team members.

Just for Fun

Most simply, a project is a defined set of activities with a clear start and end, with clear milestones and objectives, but the truth is, too many projects end up being just for fun—or maybe they were not so much fun—and end up not serving a substantive purpose. The returns for these projects might include some fun, entertainment, or just passing the time. I used to love solving jigsaw puzzles as a kid. I'd go to the store and find a puzzle that I thought was sufficiently challenging and bring it home. I planned my time and the space I needed, which was usually the kitchen table. I'd have to hurry if I used that table, so it was completed before dinner. Depending on the size of the puzzle, that was tough to do. If you've done puzzles before, you probably know the strategy: start with the edges first and then get a perfect rectangle filled. Then I'd look for the most prominent colors and group those pieces together and start to connect them. I'd proceed with other distinguishable parts of the puzzle and fit the larger groupings together until it was complete.

This was a great challenge and great fun. Even as a young person, I was practicing project management with the objective of connecting every puzzle piece so that the inspiring picture was clear and complete. I had a clear step-by-step plan to do the work. Sometimes my siblings tried to help, and since my collaboration skills were not very finely tuned at that time, they were quickly subjected to my method and plan. If they decided to stray from the plan and try a different approach to fitting pieces together, I reminded them quickly what they needed to do next to follow my plan, or I pushed their hand away or, like brothers do, insulted them! The sad truth was that no matter how great my project-management skills were, or how quickly, efficiently, and effectively the puzzle was completed, once it was done, my mom told me to clean it up and put the puzzle back in the box. All that hard work gave way to dozens of puzzle pieces, once again, broken apart and placed back in the box. Of course, I learned some skills—like how to pay attention to details, how to instruct team members about the process, and how to persist until the project was done. However, once it was all said and done, there was no enduring benefit from having completed it. The project was an exercise in entertainment and a way to pass the time.

Sadly, in countless organizations, leaders facilitate many projects that are like my puzzle-solving days. Countless hours are spent on projects that don't materialize anything enduring for the organization and fail to bring the organization closer to achieving the goals of the strategic plan or accomplishing the vision. As a result, it is important that leaders understand how to think stepwise, starting with the vision, crafting the strategic plan, determining the finances and budget, developing the right team, and then mapping out the requisite projects that will yield the outcomes your organization needs.

Once that path is followed, a leader can begin to map out a project. The Lego brand has created products for nearly one hundred years and promotes hours and weeks of orderly, creative work. Whether the builder is constructing a fire truck or a building, they do an impressive job of laying out the project in the instructions. It offers an interesting master class on project management. If you've ever opened a Lego box and set it aside, with the picture of the finished project in full view, you already know what the next step is. You open the plastic bags of sorted pieces and place them in separate piles. Then you pull out the instructions and follow them step-by-step. The box even provides the estimated ages that can execute the challenge and the estimated time it will take to build it.

Project Management

It would be so gratifying if every project at our organization had such a clear vision for what the finished project should look like, who should work on it, and how long it should take to get done. Of course, sometimes that is just not possible. Growth for any organization will likely require that leaders engage in new projects for which they must create a vision for a finished project that's never been attempted before! So, the leader will need to build on what is known to conceptualize and manage it well.

While a leader may not be able to provide the same level of clarity for any given project that Lego provides, there are principles to glean here. When starting a project, it is critical to paint a clear picture of what the finished project should look like. We've spent some time on that visioning piece. With respect to a project, the finished product or state should be clearly understood. Help your leaders figure out what is needed and the time required to complete the project in the right way. Time to completion includes understanding the capital, equipment, machinery, and people engaged to complete the work, so the time to completion might be variable depending upon quality of resources and experience of the team members. The known steps should be communicated early and often, with tasks assigned in accordance with team members' talent, knowledge, and skills to help meet deadlines to accomplish the goals.

There are many resources to support leaders in building their project-management capacity. There are calendaring and scheduling resources, project-management and communications software, and innumerable tactics and tools to keep teams aligned, motivated, and supported. Teach your leaders there is not just one key element to successful project execution. Overall, it is the responsibility of the leader to sort these elements and gauge the team's and the project's needs, always keeping the outcome in mind. This careful, ongoing calibration can lead to success.

As Leaders Go, So Goes the Project

Again, the role of leadership in project management, in my view, is underestimated and undervalued. Strong leadership can ensure that projects don't get stuck by advising as needed, ensuring the right people are matched with the right roles and tasks, and making moment-by-moment adjustments to keep it on track.

The Navy SEALs have a rigorous selection process. BUD/S (Basic Underwater Demolition/SEAL) candidates engage in a task in which they break into groups to do an arduous obstacle course that includes carrying a raft and navigating various challenges. Training officers understand that it is not only the strength, endurance, or other physical characteristics of the team members that best predict the winners and losers; leadership capacity greatly influences the outcome. To prove the point, they change the race, moving the leaders to different teams. They move the leader from the first-place boat and put him with the last-place boat, and the leader from the last-place boat is moved to the winning team's boat. Frequently, the boat that was last in the previous race will beat the boat that was first.[1]

Project management is similar in that, if the tasks are the same, and the challenges alike, the right leader in place can help navigate toward a successful outcome, whereas inexperienced leadership can result in confusion and failure. Look for leaders who engage everyone and expect all team members to contribute. The Navy SEALs understand that if one member does not feel valued or is not pulling their weight, the team loses. Leaders want to keep the team focused and aligned toward the goal, and they can quickly adjust when the outcomes are in jeopardy.

First, make sure your leaders always encourage progress, even above perfection. Many projects begin with high enthusiasm and motivation from the group—like when a young person sees a fresh new Lego box and can't wait to tear it open, see the shiny pieces, gaze at the picture of the finished product, and hop in. If there is any difficulty, however, it can be easy to lose steam. Leaders keep the end in mind and help others stay motivated and know how to prevent frustrations and distractions.

Build Up the Toolbox

To help with progress, there are a great many tools to call on in a leader's toolbox. Strong project managers break projects down into bite-size pieces, pausing to recognize small successes and wins when various milestones are reached. Technology program managers do this by creating two-week "sprints" toward a multiyear project. They host and facilitate check-ins along the way and celebrate successes as intermediate milestones are met. This is effective for many reasons. It helps the team have short-term goals to focus on when the long-term goal seems far or intangible. It also allows time for recalibration and to check the work to ensure that the project is headed in the right direction.

Another technique is to establish a template, test the template, expand the test, and then fully roll it out. Early in my career, I worked for a Christmas lighting company. We built Christmas and holiday displays. Each year, we strategized ways to expand our offerings. It would be simple if we could simply think up an idea, have the idea mass produced, and be assured of success. However, anyone who has manufactured anything will tell you it does not work that way. There can be design errors that impact production or the product simply looks bad when finished, and consequently, it never sells to the degree you expect. One way to mitigate this disappointing outcome is to follow these four phases for the project: create a template, test the template, expand the test, and build and roll out the product.

First, we developed a new lighting design and invited feedback. We talked with current and potential customers and redesigned based upon feedback, creating something we thought could work. Then a fabricator made a template. We adjusted the template several times prior to moving to the test phase. In the test phase, we put together a display for the showroom to get feedback from potential customers and foot traffic to gauge the viability of the product. Then we expanded the test, completing a house installation to show at night, took pictures, and invited feedback within a real environment. Finally, after these steps were completed, we analyzed the data based upon other launches and experiences to build out the offering and order the expected quantity at a price we could expect to sell it. Time and again, this process helped boost the likelihood of success of the product. Making decisions in haste without creating a sound project-management approach to a new initiative meant that we would not see the hoped-for financial or customer satisfaction returns.

Leaders who steer groups of people on any project must recognize that their abilities will greatly impact the success or failure of the project. Help your leaders recognize that if they see immediate and assured success in the methods, approach, and resourcing, they can adjust and respond by using a sprint method—accelerating the work—to maintain momentum. They can use the project template and then go through test, expand, and build phases as a framework for safeguarding the success of a project involving a new initiative that they want to introduce to the market.

As you identify and develop leaders, focus on developing capacity in the five critical areas. Ensure your leaders can first craft a vision of the future. It is critical to the long-term success of any organization or initiative. If you do not develop this ability in your selected leaders, it is very easy to get off track and lose sight of the purpose and objectives. Then help them think and act strategically. Leaders know that a vision remains just that without a plan. A well-crafted plan is necessary to make progress toward your desired goals. Develop leaders around financial acumen, balancing finances and budgets with enduring, long-term value of decisions for the organization and for people. Help your leaders build their capacity to build up teams, starting with self-awareness and self-development. Then ensure you equip them to manage projects by starting with clear expectations, encouraging improvement, and establishing what success looks like. There is a cyclical rhythm of developing vision, strategic planning, financial acumen, team development, and project-management capacities among leaders. If you focus on these, you will be on your way to having enduring leadership that supports the sustainability of your organization.

SECTION FOUR

Where in the Organization Can Leaders Grow?

Leadership is not about a title. It is about actions and responsibilities. It's about capacity, experience, and skills. In our organization, there is a combination of so-called soft skills and hard skills that are associated with the various roles. Our organization has a fairly traditional hierarchy because it helps facilitate clarity with roles and expectations and communicates a path for leaders to learn and grow. As you identify and develop leaders, keep in mind the kinds of capacities required for different roles, beginning with **associates, managers, directors, VPs or other executives, and, finally, C-suite-level leaders.**

CHAPTER 15

Associate

The first-level role in most organizations, whether it is a blue- or white-collar context, is generally referenced as an "associate" role. Associates are individual contributors who do not have responsibility for the work or performance of other team members. They carry out the organization's core work and activities and, in some roles, have direct interaction with customers and clients.

Valuable Contributors

Typically, associates are early in their career, or they find they prefer to remain at that level. Some organizations require certifications or credentials of some kind to advance to a manager or other role. An associate may have a predictable work routine and defined tasks. Roles might include a cashier at a grocery store, a waiter at a restaurant, or a greeter or host at a sporting event. In some sectors, associate-level roles require skills that can be learned quickly, but at other organizations, associate-level roles might require certain technical expertise, depending upon the industry. Typically, associates do not have significant decision-making responsibilities concerning the future or direction of the organization at large, but of course, their work and contributions are critical to the organization's success.

Many of an organization's employees are, of course, associate-level roles. Help your leaders learn to understand and review all work that must be accomplished by associates to have a highly functioning, high-performing organization. They should learn to determine the frequency and duration of these tasks and whether they are completed hourly, daily, or weekly. They will need to ensure there is a well-defined process and steps for completing it, as well as a clear job description for each associate.

It is important that leaders with responsibility for associates be able to match team members with roles they are well suited for. The organization might need people who enjoy predictability or repetition. Or associates might need to be strong helpers or thrive with routine and less variability. One of my favorite jobs was an associate-level role. I was a laborer for a concrete block–laying company in high school. It was my job to deliver the concrete blocks to the block layers and ensure they had the mixed cement required to lay the blocks. The blocks were delivered in stacks. I carried them from point A to point B and set them up for the block layers to access. I liked the work because it took little concentration. I could let my mind wander, listen to the music I wanted to, and get my workout done all at the same time. I left work feeling accomplished. I got stronger each day and got paid well, and it was rewarding to see tangible progress at the end of the day as the basements were built. It was the right work for me at the right time.

Engagement and Work

Unfortunately, data indicate many employees are not always satisfied and engaged with their work. Gallup employee engagement data suggests only about one-third of employees are engaged—enthusiastic, committed, and involved—with their work.[1] Great managers are needed to help keep employees engaged, which we will revisit in the following chapter. I appreciated my work in associate-level roles, especially because I could typically leave work at work and not think too much about the next day's responsibilities, as the site manager and other leaders needed to do.[2]

Additionally, lots of options exists for these roles in an array of different sectors in large cities and towns in the US. The unemployment rate has remained relatively low in recent years—currently sitting at about 4 percent as of this writing, depending on the state,[3] and many employers are urgently trying to hire associates. My role was certainly physically taxing, as some associate-level roles can be, so those won't be suitable for all potential workers. It isn't particularly mentally taxing, which, again, was great for me at the time, and is the kind of work that some will welcome, such as students or others with multiple jobs and/or other responsibilities.

Many people do aspire to move beyond an associate-level role for an array of reasons, including increased pay, the desire to take on additional challenges, or wanting to learn specialized tasks that require additional knowledge and skills. Those who want to ascend to a higher level within an organization indeed need to learn more and different tasks and acquire different skills. They have more responsibilities for their own, and often others', work, and they are accountable for different, higher standards of performance.

It is easy to see the shift in responsibilities from an associate- to a leader-level role for some industries. Namely, if you eat out at a restaurant and there is something unacceptable with the food or the service, if you bring it to the attention of the waiter, often they will get their manager to engage with you. This, of course, is because the manager has additional training, experience, responsibility, and authority to analyze and respond to customers' needs. The manager is aware of all the steps to get the food to the table, giving them an overview of what it takes to make and serve food for guests and creating desired outcomes for the restaurant overall while the associate can work on their own task of serving customers.

First-Hand Experience

Some people bring far too much ego to their management or other leadership roles, thinking that they are above the associate role and don't need to ever do that work. If you've observed such behavior, you know the damage that such a perspective brings to the culture and engagement of a workplace. Often, it is easy to see when managers or leaders have never worked an associate-level job. They don't understand the needs that their employees have and what they experience in a day, making them less capable of creating a work environment that can help them be successful. I would even say, in my observation, that those who haven't served at an associate level are limited in their capacity to lead. Their capacity is stymied at least one level below the level they aspire to achieve within the organization. The education sector follows this, with aspiring principals being required to serve up to five years as teachers in the classroom prior to leading a building. In business, if an individual wants to be a vice president but was never an associate, and perhaps stepped right into a management role out of college, they may not advance beyond a director role, and it might initially be tough to figure out why. For me, however, it is obvious: It is because they have

Associate

never worked an associate-level job. For some of these leaders, they lack the experience and thereby lack understanding of the people and operations that can inform their decision-making.

Help leaders understand that associate-level roles are extremely valuable and critical to the success of any organization and will help support their own success if they gain experience in those roles. Associate-level work helps build understanding of the power and value of performing the basics, the core operations, and the ins and outs of the organization. They sometimes work closely with people who are both internal and external to the organization, and experience the ways the systems and processes impact those people in ways that leaders might overlook if they've not seen it firsthand.

Author Robert Fulghum reminds us that all we really need to know, it turns out, we learned in kindergarten.[4] Simple and timeless lessons about how to treat people and things, how to observe and listen, how to be responsible for yourself and others, how to enjoy simple things, how to stay safe and healthy, how to be prepared, etc., are all things young humans practice in kindergarten. I think Fulghum's credo, shared decades ago, still has wisdom for us today. These are some of the very things you will learn and practice in an associate-level—and frankly, any—role within most organizations.

Organizations are fraught with disconnected leaders who make decisions at the top that affect the lives and livelihoods of associates, and too often those decisions are at the expense of their employees. Most associates, of course, must work. They need the paycheck, so if the environment is bad, they may quit and go someplace else to work. But it might be even worse if they quit and stay—so-called quiet quitting, which may be more about poor management than it is about bad employees.[5] When disgruntled employees stay at the organization, they often spread that disengagement and mistrust, and it blunts the progress and productivity of the organization. There is an epidemic of disengagement in the American workforce, and it is a direct result, in my view, of far too many disconnected leaders who have never worked as associates. They ascend the ladder quickly but fail to connect with and understand the needs of the (approximately) 70 percent of the workforce who are not engaged.[6] In my experience, it is important to find and hire people who are not chasing a title but instead are ready to set and achieve goals and grow in their role.

As a leader intent on developing leaders, recognize the power of developing routine, clearly defined tasks for associates. Create an engaging environment where their workplace needs are met. Create the kind of culture where associates are valued and understood. If an associate seems disengaged, look at the manager first to see if and how the culture is fracturing. Disengagement, in my opinion, doesn't start at the bottom. It trickles down from the top or because of leadership decisions that negatively impact associates. As you identify and develop leaders, make sure they understand the contributions and value that associates bring to the organization. The degree to which they understand may well correlate with their capacity to advance and lead in the future.

CHAPTER 16

Manager

As you develop leaders, remind them that setting an environment that promotes success is the job of the manager. Managers in our organization are tasked with supervising daily activities and outcomes, assigning goals and following established standards, and using policies to provide guidance to associates. Where the largest number of roles within most organizations are at the associate level, the organization thrives or withers at the management level. Gallup studies of managers show that about 70 percent of the variance in employee engagement can be attributed to the manager.[1] If a leader enters the workforce in a management-level role, they only know what it takes to get work done theoretically and might not fully understand and appreciate the associates' experiences and their needs. Encourage leaders to get experience alongside associates, so they can lead them well.

The Best Managers Meet Needs

Managers are responsible for helping to meet their team's needs, so they can best do their work. At worst, an inexperienced manager may take for granted those who serve as associates and fail to connect with them, and ultimately, the team can become disengaged with their work and the organization. Employee disengagement costs US companies billions in lost productivity every year, so getting the manager equation right is critical.[2] While not every management and leadership challenge is fixed by having previous experience at the associate level, you do increase the likelihood that the manager understands and appreciates what associates do in a day and the ways they keep the organization humming and moving forward.

Associates will either quit the organization, remain at the same level with little growth, remain at the same level but with some learning or expanded responsibility, or they may promote to a management level within the organization based upon the work of their manager and the manager's capacity to develop themselves and their team members. Even organizations with the clearest vision and committed associates can only grow to the extent that their managers are able to facilitate it. Poor management stifles employee growth and stunts organizational productivity.[3]

A manager, for the context of this book, understands what work needs to be done and when work needs to be done. They understand goals and targets that teams need to hit for the organization to function well. They are familiar with workflow processes. And as stated, most importantly, managers know what their team members need to do their work well. They sometimes train, establish expectations, and help hold team members accountable. They are ready to coach their team members if growth is needed. Great managers frequently spot and recognize good work and help establish the culture and mood of the workplace. Managers care about the development of their associates and are not just taskmasters.

Manager

Managers effectively resource the work to team members to help make progress toward big-picture goals and monthly targets. Great managers know the strengths and weaknesses of their team and match tasks with that talent to help facilitate the best outcomes. They have strong attention to project details to ensure that all work is covered. The best managers think ahead to the next steps and have considered contingency plans, if something goes awry.[4]

As you train leaders, again, they might begin leading at a manager level. So, you want to ensure that you have managers who truly value people and the work of helping them be their best. Appointing the right managers will be one of the best business decisions you make. Find managers who relish coaching but don't long to be the boss.[5]

As people have chosen to be part of your organization and are following the leadership of their managers, it is important to know the processes and the plans they need to be successful. Additionally, managers need to be adept at adjusting as the unexpected comes up. People's lives shift and move, as does the environment and context that the organization is operating within. Managers will need to keep the mission central and be prepared to adjust as needed.

A Recipe for Success

Now that you're a bit more grounded in the role of the manager, it is time to dive into the process of building their needed skills. They need to be attuned to measurement and indicators of success, find ways to engage and motivate their teams, be present and visible, and be prepared to make tough decisions.

It is important to think about practical ways for managers to grow their team and hit monthly goals and targets. There is a popular adage that says what gets measured gets improved. New managers need to ensure that the tasks that are recurring—on an hourly, daily, weekly, or monthly basis—have a process in place to measure progress. Additionally, managers will reference those metrics and use them to adjust people or processes to help improve the output. Measures include production measures and indicators, as well as people measures, that help shed light on the extent to which the manager has a strong, engaged workplace culture among the team.

There is a familiar anecdote about businessman Charles Schwab who used friendly competition to boost motivation and productivity among his teams.[6] He took a simple approach. At the end of the day shift, he wrote a number 6 on the ground in chalk as the workers left for the day.

As the team exited the plant, they passed the second shift team entering the building. The teams asked why a 6 was written on the ground. The manager noted that 6 was the number of items manufactured by the day shift. He then left for the day. The next morning, when the team arrived back at the plant, the 6 was crossed out and a 7 was written next to it. I'm sure you can see where this story is going. Shift productivity increased, until both shifts were consistently hitting many more items manufactured per shift. While competition isn't necessarily the primary or only lever that a manager can pull to help inspire strong performance, in this case, team members achieved more of their potential. Strong managers and leaders will recognize and celebrate such wins and improvement with their teams.

The story is a simple illustration of the power of measurement and identifying ways to motivate and inspire teams to produce strong outcomes. The manager understood how teams can be galvanized around a process and a goal. There was one focus, one goal. Teams appreciate clarity around a defined goal. The tactic served to help each team member think about what they do to enable completion of the process and how their improvement drives overall improvement. Generally, the manager aimed to create more energy and positivity and helped to build focus and efficiency overall.

Ready to Help

Managers understand that every team is different, and every person is motivated by different things. What works for one team may not work for another necessarily. But all strong managers evaluate the team's work and productivity, clarify the goals for themselves and their team members, then seek ways to bring out the best work in each person. Part of our business involves conducting vehicle security patrols at planned times throughout the night. Sometimes different drivers on the same route complete the route with varying degrees of speed, efficiency, and attentiveness. Some drivers complete all planned stops in just a few hours, with a high degree of care and attention, while others take twice as many hours to complete the stops, and their work is not as thorough. Good managers realize that a strong performance isn't always about the time the task takes, though that can be important. And it is always about the team member's work and effort.

When I managed a team early in my career, I knew that the team could do better. I called a team meeting, and I set a goal for security patrols for the night. One vocal leader on the team said my goal could not be achieved. I clarified the expectation once again. The shift leader indicated they would not follow through on my expectation. The plan I had made was a critical starting point for the success of the business. I let the shift leader know that if they were not able or willing to follow through on the plan that they needed to find another place to work. There was a challenge from that shift leader because they perceived I had no other option than to have them work and patrol throughout the night. However, I let them know that I planned to do the patrol in their absence. I got a uniform and followed through on that task because our customer expected the work to be done and done well. It was a pivotal moment, and the tide turned quickly around what the expectations for work would be. I certainly did not do the work perfectly that night, but I think the team enjoyed coaching me on the details and the ins and outs of their work. The team knew that the work needed to improve and that I was willing to roll up my sleeves to support and help make it happen. The culture of our team changed that day. The work was done better, and the team was more engaged and prouder of their work.

Perhaps the most important element to this story, though, was the fact that, as a manager, not only did I clarify the expectation, but I was also willing to join the group in helping make it happen. While the manager's primary role is to set their team members up for success, if you set a goal for them that you are unwilling to tangibly support, you might struggle to receive the respect of your team. However, your hard work and willingness to work alongside at critical moments can help them sustain strong, high-level performance over time.

Restaurants are always an interesting place to watch this happen in real time. I often look around to see if I can spot the manager and see how they engage with their team and/or with customers. In some establishments, it's tough to spot the manager because they're not present or, even if they are, they aren't necessarily identifiable as the manager. At some locations, you can spot the manager hopping in to serve and support the team, even busing tables or bringing out condiments or other items to customers. I think this presence is a boost for the team, as they see that they have the support of their manager. While the manager certainly can't accomplish all the work, they can model, help, support, and observe what is needed for everyone—team members and customers—to have a positive experience. As you think about calling on new leaders, look for those willing to be a working manager—one who is a student of the tasks of the team. The best managers listen, learn, and respond to their team's needs. They know how and when to assist and encourage a positive, engaged workplace.

Managers have a tough job and sometimes need to make tough decisions. The leaders that you develop must learn their team is watching them and assessing the impact on their work experience. That impact is generally the way they understand leadership effectiveness. They are watching how the leader acts and whether they value those who do a good job and are willing to support them. They will notice when the manager gives more attention and time to those who are not performing well. Worse, the team will suffer if someone is allowed to persist in their poor behaviors that impact other members. There is a difference between a critical, hard-working employee and one who is a vocal, low-performing naysayer who does not contribute to the team's success. A manager will lose credibility with the team if such behavior is tolerated for too long. It will erode the manager's capacity to effect change and lead. Effective managers know and advocate for strong processes, they are willing to support and tangibly help as needed, and they recognize and celebrate strong performance.

An important leadership skill, even at the managerial level, is the decision to facilitate someone's exit from your organization. Helping your leaders learn to do this professionally is important and needed to maintain high productivity and a positive team culture. If you do not have a leader willing to support that kind of environment, help your leaders beware the temptation to keep a person on their team only because there's a role that needs to be filled. The harm to the team can be greater if they stay than if they go. Sometimes, if a highly negative person exits the organization, the work of the smaller team might improve as morale and focus improve.

As a leader looking to identify and develop leaders, find those who have a service-oriented mindset. Find those who are willing to hop in and help and can demonstrate what strong performance looks like. Then be sure that the manager understands the metrics that indicate success and the process needed to achieve them. The potential for leadership grows within your organization as you identify and select the right managers!

CHAPTER 17

Director

In our traditional organizational structure, we also have directors. As you identify leaders and develop them, understand that different skills and experiences are required for director-level leaders than are required for managers. Teach your developing leaders that directors need additional strategic thinking capacity and the ability to respond and initiate changes in response to quarterly and annual metrics and milestones. They help build and oversee the implementation of processes and systems or adjust them, as required. They help empower their managers and teams to do their work and accomplish the organization's aims.

The Daily for Directors

Directors need to evaluate layers of information across different systems. Namely, they need to understand and assess the resources required across technology, facilities, or other infrastructure, in addition to talent and skills needed to determine the best processes to accomplish the milestones and reach goals. They need to be able to gauge progress, identify measures of success, and appoint the best managers to meet the needs of their team members. They need to be able to coach managers. They need to learn to provide support for their managers' decisions and jointly set performance expectations. Directors create an environment that allows managers and associates to be successful.

Teach your leaders that there are other less tangible, but critical, leadership areas that directors might need to develop. They provide stability and consistency in the workplace, modeling excellence in accountability and performance. They analyze each element that influences team performance, looking for ways to help their teams consistently perform well. When they spot challenges in workflow or performance, they must be able to identify possible solutions and determine the best one. When their decisions and choices prove to be ineffective, they need to be responsive, and course correct. Like managers, their communication in managing change will be tested and honed. They know when to include other leaders and when to invite managers and team members to inform the development of those changes.

Over the years, I've taken several trips to Ecuador with our kids to support some home-building projects. Each time we are there, I've been so impressed with the work and leadership of the project director. The bilingual director serves as a bridge between the short-term service team and the local families and team members. In addition to leading in the bicultural context, they must build operations and processes with resources and timelines that allow for efficient and effective construction.

The director is skilled in creating processes that support the people who are working, while keeping the very tangible objectives top

Director

of mind, namely that of completing a home-building project within a given time frame. I think, rightly, the director focuses first and foremost on the people and their needs. He identifies a family to serve with the home-building project and then secures the team members, who typically travel to Quito for the work. The days and times are established, and he arranges necessary transportation for people and supplies. The director creates the building milestones and timelines for managers to follow. The director understands the vision and purpose for the work and develops a plan and a team to help facilitate the work. Once the project is underway, the director communicates with managers and team members to ensure the project is moving along as planned.

The director is also a servant of the team, providing support to ensure that others can work well and even enjoy their work. I've observed the small things and big things that the director does to support managers and associates along the way. The director pays close attention to what people like and appreciate, providing snacks and treats. I remember one member saying they like vanilla sandwich cookies with ice cream. The director made sure to provide a snack basket and an ice cream stop at the end of each day. Careful attention to those small details about people can build team engagement, especially since managers know that the director is willing to create the environment needed for all to have a great experience and be successful.

Directors have a responsibility to create processes that support consistently strong performance with few hurdles for teams. If those systems are in place, it allows managers to manage with little chaos and fewer stops and starts. The director in Ecuador accomplishes this and demonstrates the consistencies at the jobsite. The homes are typically constructed in rural areas, which have few resources available. Before the building begins, the building plans are created and communicated. Lots are measured. And the required materials and supplies are ordered and delivered daily so that the time and hours are well spent, and nothing is missed. The time of workers and volunteers is always maximized. One of the most challenging materials to transport and manage are concrete blocks. The project generally takes hundreds of these blocks, which must be loaded and unloaded by hand. The director knows it is a grueling exercise but is attentive to that time to create camaraderie and take care of the people doing the work. He also creates a most workable process that helps alleviate the difficulty. The team lines up, then the blocks are passed down the line and stacked neatly at the final destination, where they will be used to build a wall. The director doesn't wait for others to step up to do the work but instead takes the spot at the front of the line. He kicks off the process, handing the blocks off to the next person in line and adjusting if there seems to be a bottleneck. Within just a few minutes, the blocks are off-loaded and stacked where they need to be. It is satisfying to see these foundational materials ready to go. The best part, of course, is taking a snack and water break!

The director at the house site can't be effective if they continually are trying to do—or redo—the work of their team members. However, they work to balance participating in the work and being present to support the team with the time required to plan and adjust processes as needed. The director typically spends an hour working directly with the team to see and listen to the needs and decide any adjustments that are needed.

Directors within our organization have responsibility and accountability for similar things. From the moment that new team members are onboarded, the director communicates with them, informing about the processes necessary to accomplish the quarterly goals. The director also informs them of the measures for success and what team members do to help facilitate them. They take care to routinely evaluate those metrics and advise managers about how to help teams make needed adjustments. They facilitate and manage change when new infrastructure or technological advances are added or when team members or project direction changes. The director works with managers to evaluate the skills and experiences of the team members and associates to align work and tasks well. They often design and facilitate a regular cadence of meetings and project reviews to ensure they have the pulse of the team and a clear line of sight on the project progress.

As already described, the director has an important role in designing and adjusting workflow processes. Team members deserve to have the materials and resources they need to do their work, including access to the managers and infrastructure that will enable their skills and talent to shine. Directors recruit and appoint managers who can assist with leveraging that talent and skill and align it with the resources to help create the best possible workplace.

As a director develops a sustainable process, they must account for an array of internal and external variables with people and products. The director should be able to refine the pathway to setting up the process, setting clear and reasonable expectations with dates, times, and milestones. In partnership with project managers, if the project has additional team members for ongoing support, the right team members are then invited to execute the work with clarity about the tasks and milestones they are responsible for completing and by when.

Managing Change

It could be challenging for you to help a new leader learn to simultaneously consider so many variables and data points in assessing and steering work processes and systems. Additionally, even when leaders learn to identify and assess those variables, and gain enough experience needed to create and amend those processes to facilitate success, it is critical to manage the changes well with the team.

Change-management experts have helped to make resources available that support leaders in this critical area. Fundamentally, a director and management team must develop and implement an intentional and detailed communication plan—as part of a larger change-management plan—prior to, throughout, and following any process or structure change. It is a critical and often overlooked step in leadership development that can help ensure the best opportunity for success. You have probably been part of organizations that made a change—practically overnight—with the belief that ripping off the proverbial bandage for the change was the way to go. Then employees, and maybe even some leaders, were surprised by it. In many instances where the change was not well managed, it extended the time to full adoption and blunted the ability of teams to develop competency with the new process and work. When the change approach is poorly managed, it can make the experience bad for all parties. While the plan and change may well be best for the organization, the poor change and communication flub can stymie the success of the initiative.

Leaders—particularly those in a director role, who are potentially involved in designing significant changes for their division or department—must be carefully coached in the value and work of communication and its role in managing change. Sometimes the urgency of the initiative and the turnaround time for implementation results in tabling work done to communicate and advise team members about the purpose and new process. Sometimes leaders are simply excited and eager to get something "fixed" and, again, miss the necessary step of planning the rollout with their teams. Well-trained leaders in a director role keep the long-term value and opportunity in mind as they implement new initiatives, and this long view informs the communication plan that can help facilitate success.

I follow a communications framework that has been helpful in making the rollout of new initiatives more successful. First, I communicate the vision and intent for the change. I clarify points of purpose about the outcomes we need to accomplish. I next connect the current initiative to the strategic plan to underscore that there is an intended purpose and order to the work and the way that the new process and work will help accelerate achievement of our stated goals. I next review the requisite finances and resources so that the teams know there is care and intentionality in weighing the costs and potential benefits, acknowledging risk level (if relevant) rather than shying away from that conversation. Next, I discuss the power inherent in the team members to support the introduction and adoption of the change. Last, I assign the projects to the managers and teams to get the necessary tasks done.

As our business continues to grow, the work of change and initiating and implementing new processes is ongoing. The communications framework is repeated frequently and to varying levels of intensity depending on the initiative—from technology upgrades to organizational structure adjustments, to new sales or employee onboarding processes, to budget and finance management. A small, but not insignificant, example of this concerns shuffling desks and furniture as the company grows and departments and personnel are updated. In the early years, I overlooked the need to account for the concern team members had around moving desks and changing workstations. We have expanded within our office building and often reconfigure the movable walls and furniture to accommodate new team members or to make better use of our limited space. The process of moving desks around still happens up to a few times each year. At first, team members were really concerned about why they were being moved and wondered about the implications for their work. People sometimes had hurt feelings and expressed complaints or even fear that the change had something to do with their personal performance when they were informed that they were changing areas or desks.

It took me too long to acknowledge that the failure to communicate about the change was a leadership failure. I learned and realized—albeit the hard way—that you should not start the conversation by saying, "Tomorrow you will report to your new workstation and desk right over there on the east side of the building." (I realize how that sounds now!) In my mind, communicating the information in a concise way was efficient, but it was most certainly not the most effective. The frustration was palpable for teams and impacted productivity.

I began to implement a more intentional six-week communication cycle around changes in office configurations. Other initiatives may require a different duration for the communication cycle. Six weeks prior to the change, I begin to communicate the vision for the change and why it is needed. I discuss growth that has happened and the ways we're anticipating it and responding to it. I describe where I see the business going and the ways we are fulfilling our purpose as an organization. Then I discuss the ways we will continue to grow and work and how the office and layout need to adjust to accommodate those next steps for the organization. In the next week, I communicate how the change is informed by the strategic plan and how it will enable us to accomplish the goals that were set, and I connect those details to ways we're expanding and organizing our structure to inform new hires. Then I speak to the details about where those team members will be set up in the building. Per the framework, I discuss the finance and budget and the value anticipated by initiating the updates, which often require additional materials, equipment, and software to accommodate the new hires and ensure the teams have the stuff and the space they need to do the work. At week four prior to the change, I communicate final logistics about where individuals will sit and how teams will be situated. A fair amount of thinking is spent here in partnership with the directors and managers now, as both people and process needs are included in those conversations. In the fifth week of the cycle, I discuss upcoming projects that might be impacted by the reconfiguration. Then, finally, on the sixth week—right before the moves happen—our leaders show employees where they will be and reveal the map or plan. Then when the move happens, some teams have a small celebration of the successful move to help create a positive vibe for the new work and location.

This might seem like a lot of work—and frankly, it is—and we certainly don't hit every step perfectly every time we make a change. But spending this time communicating, especially when there's so much heavy lifting to do, helps drastically improve the whole process. Many people even like the anticipation and feel impatient for it to happen, as the vision feels exciting and clear and will ultimately benefit individuals and the organization overall. In recent years, we have had to move people and stuff quite frequently so that now, such change is our modus operandi. Complaints and pain points are certainly still there, but as we have become better at anticipating those pain points, we address them early and often.

It is amazing to see the ways that structured communication from the leaders have made such a big difference. With vision, purpose, and clear expectations established early and often, the final reveal of the process and logistics goes more smoothly, and productivity picks up more quickly once it is completed. When this level of care happens, the negative emotions that surround the change dissipate more quickly because team members are considered and respected in the process. When concerns arise, they are discussed and addressed, and employees get to know their new neighbors and establish working relationships well.

LEAD EXPONENTIALLY

As you develop leaders who have capacity to oversee departments in a traditional director role with managers and several (or many) associate-level team members reporting to them, it is important for them to be able to evaluate systems and processes that enable the organization to achieve its goals consistently. These leaders must have ways to analyze processes, identify opportunities to facilitate outcomes, and be prepared to make recommendations for changes and updates. Then, the best leaders must grow in their capacity to communicate change and be responsive to the needs and concerns of the team members that are impacted by change. A director needs to be aware of the ways people might respond when abrupt changes are made and the ways that engagement takes a hit if teams feel disrespected and not included in the work.

In our organization, again, which has a more traditional organizational structure, we next have a vice president role that requires other leadership capacities to experience success.

CHAPTER 18

Vice President

Fewer leaders will continue in their careers to an executive-level role at the senior executive or VP level. As someone who develops leaders, you will want to understand the shifting capacities and responsibilities for this role. Generally, there is more responsibility for managing the direction and future of the organization at the vice president level. In our organization, vice presidents translate strategy into plans for execution and develop the processes and systems that enable execution of the strategy. It is sometimes more challenging for these leaders to maintain connections with individual contributors and associates, so they must be attentive to maintaining a culture of trust and openness across the organization.

Expanded Responsibility

As you develop leaders who are candidates for executive-level leadership, you must consider additional skills—and temperament—that help facilitate success. For this chapter, I'll share a framework to build expertise to avoid the potential pitfalls for senior-level leaders. The vice president role, which might be a senior executive director or other title in some organizations, is a senior-level leader who maintains responsibility for securing resources and ensuring accomplishment of the vision. These leaders have a heightened responsibility for framing and accomplishing the strategic plan, and they must have elevated financial acumen. While directors also need financial acumen, they will also need to spend more time and attention on team development. Managers will tend to focus more on team development and project management. Executive leaders must be able to think strategically, have sound decision-making skills, and, again, have refined and tested financial acumen. To do this, they must build their expertise. They must be aware of the proverbial blanks in their knowledge bank and work to fill in those blanks.

It is important that leaders who have the ability to assume executive leadership roles be prepared for the amplified work intensity that their responsibility and authority will likely create. It is critical for these leaders to demonstrate stability and engender trust via their decisions and communications. Some who assume this level feel accomplished and enjoy additional pay and personal professional accomplishment; however, some in the role underestimate the increased accountability and expectations. It is important to operate, communicate, and process information thoroughly and, sometimes, quickly. The decisions made affect the lives of many more people at multiple layers of the organization. It is important to have leaders at this level who recognize and manage stress effectively. In some circumstances or businesses, there can be some continual stress applied in the pursuit of time-bound revenue or sales goals, or when there are significant events and programs being initiated. It is important to be able to maintain stability and have healthy approaches to coping with and managing stress.

Along with other researchers, author Jeffrey Pfeffer—in his book *Dying for a Paycheck*—has quantified the ways that stress leads to health challenges for those experiencing workplace stress.[1] Those in positions of leadership who have significant accountability also have stress as a frequent companion. It is important for the few leaders who aspire to senior leadership roles to understand exactly what they are aspiring to. They must have the requisite experience and tools to respond to the additional intensity involved with the role, as well as recognize the stress they can potentially or accidentally cause those they are leading.[2]

Leaders at the executive level must be able and prepared to assume responsibility for what happens in the organization. They should be averse to placing blame for missteps and own them instead. Ownership grows as leadership responsibility grows and expands. For those who are less prepared when they assume this kind of role, it can be easy to default to finding scapegoats. Some leaders can make the mistake of being hyper focused on achieving this level of leadership and want to get there quickly, while overlooking the critical leadership lessons and growth opportunities required to succeed in the role. Some who get there before they have had adequate development opportunities may be vulnerable to ego and a sense of entitlement and perceived perks that come with such roles in some organizations. But while ambition can be a motivating characteristic to ascending to such a role, be sure to seek those leaders who actively pair growth and learning alongside their ambition. Identify and develop those who express their ambition by humbly and actively learning. As you identify potential executive leaders, remember that past performance is always the best indicator of potential future success.

LEAD EXPONENTIALLY

Help your leaders aspiring to an executive leader role to continue homing in on specific elements to learn and grow. Encourage them to develop expertise around their organization's sector, the market, and other technical capacities. It can be tempting for successful leaders who have ascended the proverbial corporate ladder to think they have learned or seen it all. However, entitlement and ego must be continually checked at the door and replaced with a commitment to ongoing learning and growth and finding those who bring expertise and skill within the lanes that are most needed in the organization. Successful executives model the value of learning and refuse to give in to the temptation of entitlement that sometimes accompanies the title.

Effective vice presidents or other executive leaders are excellent strategic thinkers who can translate strategy to actionable steps. They think about where to allocate budget and finances such that they have the best opportunity to achieve organizational-level goals. They also spot weaknesses and challenges in process or productivity and make business decisions that address those challenges.

Vice presidents and other executives are strong scenario thinkers, which, ideally, is rooted in experience and observation. They understand the potential implications for various decisions. They can assess both the forest and the trees and see all parts of the picture to make the most informed decision that is best for the business. It can be easy to make decisions that center the executive rather than the business. Principled leaders might need to make decisions that are not necessarily comfortable for one's own division or area of work but are clearly best for the organization overall. Ensure that those leaders you identify and develop have a track record of prioritizing others and the health of the organization overall.

As I've described, my personal top priority in life is my faith. This priority helps keep me centered on the lessons learned via the life and ministry of Jesus in my decision-making. Jesus modeled servant leadership that prioritized others. If you have a leader who continually watches out for their own advancement, that pattern will be tough to change if afforded additional power over parts of the organization. Jesus's followers didn't always do this perfectly. Simon Peter fell into being self-protective and betrayed Jesus three times, but Jesus continued to believe in his potential to lead His people with a courageous, others-centered approach that Jesus modeled.[3] Following His death and resurrection, Jesus commissioned Peter to share the Gospel and care for His flock.[4]

Beware of Biases

Leaders in executive roles also need to have an awareness of various kinds of bias and the ways that they influence decision-making. Develop leaders in these areas, pointing out potential kinds of biases along the way so that your executive leaders have practice in not only recognizing that there is potential bias at work, but so they also can adjust the decision-making process to help mitigate the possible effect of those cognitive biases. Researchers inform us of the detrimental effects of leadership bias, namely poor morale driven by disrespectful behavior toward employees and customers.[5] Skilled executive leaders recognize, acknowledge, and then address their own biases and self-interest to make the right decision that is best for all involved. One way to do this is to practice thinking in the long term versus the short term. Leaders making strong strategic decisions in the moment, and those who are wisely leveraging finances and resources are determined to skate where the proverbial puck is actually going within the organization and the market, not pursuing current trends or fads that might look or feel good within a moment.

LEAD EXPONENTIALLY

You do not need to go far to find organizations that have made a series of ineffective decisions, and I wouldn't be surprised if those decisions rested at the executive—VP—level or perhaps higher. Organizations sometimes jump on a bandwagon of concepts and ideas that are mirroring some popular trend, but which are not working toward the future of their own organization specifically. Our business, as I've shared, is a franchising firm. This kind of replicative decision-making is apparent within this space. There are organization leaders looking at market leaders and trying to replicate what they see but without necessary innovations in their own sector. They attempt to leverage a price or an initiative or other strategic approach with some hubris that makes them think they will implement the initiative better. Unfortunately, too many will burn money and fall into obscurity. While Chick-fil-A, for example, has seen ongoing success as a franchising firm, it isn't possible to replicate all their success and approaches if you are going to franchise organizations within a service sector.

The danger for executives trying to replicate the approach of parallel organizations was, I think, evident in the somewhat recent retail competition of Walmart, Target, and even Kmart. Each of these three retailers were fighting to earn consumers' dollars. Walmart focused on a low-cost leadership position. They work through the supply chain to cut costs, reduce shelf space and package size, and eliminate waste and inefficiency in their model to pass the savings along to the consumer, all while maintaining some profit margin, of course.[6] Target has successfully focused on consumer experience, store formats, and ongoing attention to product design, all while maintaining a reasonable price point.[7] As a cautionary tale, Kmart did not effectively make the decisions that could keep the retailer relevant in the space. They tended to observe and respond to their competitors' price points or adjust inventory to mirror the product lines of their competitors rather than studying and understanding the ways that they could uniquely meet needs for consumers and sustain a viable market share.[8]

While executives certainly must observe and be aware about what others in their market are doing, making choices that feel safe or secure because others are doing it, and thinking those choices will be the right ones, is limiting to the business at best and might be the wrong one for the organization. You need to choose leaders who can analyze the information and make decisions that yield the expected results. Executive leaders see opportunities, understand the potential headwinds, and lean on experts to craft ways that the organization can respond to those opportunities.

Executives have experience—and expertise—and must, of course, make significant decisions. It is natural to think that expertise is built over time and with experience. And as mentioned, there is truth to that. But understand that that kind of experience and expertise can be built regardless of the title one holds. Experience comes with circumstances, so as you identify and develop potential executive leaders, know that their experiences and the ways they have grown in their understanding and expertise matter more than their tenure or their current title. Not to belabor the point, but it is important to remember that effectiveness and expertise are not a by-product of the title. Outcomes and performance that are a result of leadership decisions—especially during challenging circumstances—are the best indicator of a person's capacity and expertise. Don't overlook those who might not yet have that title, and be sure to focus on what they know and have accomplished rather than their role or title.

Expertise is sometimes built in the shadows rather than on the stage. In the shadows, or outside of the limelight, is where leaders should think, practice, plan, and contemplate. As an early leader with an aspiration to learn and grow, I often observed and reflected on the public and, as much as possible, the private decisions of key leaders. I considered their strategic decisions and the financial acumen that they demonstrated. I wanted to be able to leverage those learnings when I found myself in a similar role. As you consider a leader to invest in and develop, you could ask, generally, about the ways they learn about leadership and their decision-making process. Ask what leadership decisions they've observed and what they learned by observing them. This process of learning is evidenced often in sports. As coaches prepare for a game, they may watch tape of their own team and that of their opponents. They observe the plays and techniques and skills to create a game plan. They see what worked and what didn't for their own team and for the opposing team's previous opponents as well. Then they make decisions about the talent and resources they need to align and give their team the best chance to win. Similarly, VPs will need to review previous decisions and understand the talent and expertise and skills needed to craft and execute a plan to experience ongoing success.

As you consider a leader for a new VP or other executive-level role, look at the decisions that the predecessors in that role made. Be sure that your new leader knows about and studies those decisions. Have conversations about what worked and what didn't. And ask what they might do the same or differently in the role. Encourage that leader to study and evaluate their own and others' decisions. Do this often and be sure they have the right kind of data and information and that they are practiced at identifying what they don't know.

Encourage leaders to be self-aware about their own biases. They should be practiced at observing their peers within the organization to see how cadence and effectiveness informs their own approaches. Teach them to look outside of the organization to see what similar individuals or organizations are doing with similar resources and circumstances and analyze what is relevant. In short, executive leaders should always be observing and learning from leaders around them. The simple framework is look within, look around, and look outside. Look within and be self-aware about decisions made and potential biases held. Look around the organization to observe other leaders and ensure the vantage point is very clear, all perspectives are included, and important lessons are accounted for. Then look outside of the organization to learn from others' decisions, including their successes and missteps. Continually practicing this kind of observing and learning is critical for executive leaders to continue to make strong strategic decisions.

As a leader who wants to identify and develop leaders even at the vice president/executive level, you also should look for those who understand the expectation of ongoing growth and expanding expertise. Learn and grow in the shadows when others are not necessarily watching so that they can make strong strategic plans and decisions and do so with sound financial acumen. Look for those who can see a comprehensive view of what needs to be done and understand enough of the details to ensure that resources are most effectively appropriated toward the stated goals. Then ensure those executive leaders have the right directors in place who can pick up the work and keep their managers and teams on track in implementing the processes and tasks. A few leaders will be able to master these expectations and can step into a C-suite-level role for the organization. Let's think about some of those unique elements at this level of leadership.

CHAPTER 19

Chief Level

The highest level of leadership in many organizations with a traditional structure, including ours, is the chief level—the too-oft-coveted C-suite. Chief-level roles determine long-term strategy and organizational priorities. They create structures and develop policies to support achievement of organizational-level goals. While you may not be looking, specifically, to identify and develop leaders who aspire to this level of responsibility or who will ultimately reach it, it is necessary to understand some of the demands of the role, since decisions made at this level have such a broad impact.

Oversight and Line of Sight

There are many different areas of responsibility for the so-called C-suite, such as the CEO, who owns responsibility for the organization's health, growth, and performance; the chief financial officer; the chief operating officer; or other specialized chief-level roles, such as the chief technology, strategy, marketing, or development officer. Most are aware that the "chief" designation promotes the highest level of authority but, more importantly, is also the highest-level accountability and responsibility for the performance of the organization. An organization may have one person as the sole owner/operator who assumes the CEO title. Or you may have a large organization with a CEO and many other C-level executives with thousands of employees. The role and responsibilities are similar with respect to who has the oversight and responsibility for the organization, but, of course, the day-to-day activities, scope, and scale of the decisions can vary widely, depending on the organization. While a revered role, the title is sometimes overused.

I think that the C-level role is the most often misunderstood, so I want to try to uncover a bit of the ambiguity that sometimes surrounds C-level roles and share some of my lessons learned along the way. In my view, leaders who aspire to chief-level roles must have a desire to develop other leaders within the organization. They need to be able to develop others and help them succeed for the organization to move forward and have enduring success. While this is a skill that must be honed for any leader in any organization at any level, it is particularly true of those in the C-suite. In the role, you become most acutely aware that you cannot make informed, unilateral decisions about everything. You must rely upon the most knowledgeable and capable leaders to interpret information and advise you along the way. You must become refined at spotting those leaders. As a C-level leader, you are often responsible for external perception of the organization. You might represent the mission or brand of the organization both internally and externally.

Humility and Trust

Help your leaders understand that again, humility must accompany the C-suite leader, knowing that they possess ultimate responsibility but rely on many people to ensure the organization succeeds. Successful leaders at this level can garner attention and trust, and as they demonstrate effectiveness, the cycle of trust and responsiveness to their leadership can grow.

Again, the C-level leadership role has the highest level of authority, but also the highest level of responsibility. These leaders serve the entire organization and every internal and external stakeholder who engages or interacts with the organization. These leaders, whether they have a long or short tenure at the organization, are responsible for learning from and leveraging past lessons, while forecasting for the future. Future casting and authenticity are two important tools in the C-level leader's tool kit.

As I've mentioned, I'm personally inspired and informed by the ways that Jesus cast a vision for what life is like in His Kingdom. His preaching and teaching centered on this vision that is different from what life in a world ruled by those with selfish ambition is like. While Jesus did not lead a company or even a nonprofit, His leadership of the disciples was always an unassuming posture that centered on the Kingdom. He invited others into that Kingdom marked by reconciliation, forgiveness, love, and hope. Jesus often delivered difficult messages, especially to those who were in leadership! He let them know that they are accountable to the downcast and spoke with empathy and clarity to each audience. He did not waver, even while facing an unjust death.

Hopeful Future

I've worked hard in my role as CEO to never waver on the positive vision of the future, to maintain that vision, even when circumstances are difficult and muddy the decision-making waters. I'm grateful for the chance to invite others to a hopeful vision of the future and to maintain that vision, which can help provide thriving lives and opportunities for people to learn, grow, and live good lives. It is important to keep the organization's vision ever present and at the forefront of everyone's mind. Walt Disney had a vision for Disney World that he kept relatively under wraps, while a team of people began to acquire the land in central Florida. He wanted to transform the more than 27,000 acres to create a "Vacation Kingdom"—as it was referred to during construction in 1970—but because he passed away during development, his brother, Roy, saw the project through to completion. Of course, Disney's vision eventually came to life.[1] The space and the destination could also be free from other businesses that would encroach on the park. Obviously, Disney's detailed, well-articulated vision became reality. C-suite leaders should have a similarly clear vision, the ability to clearly communicate it, and an informed, unwavering belief in it.

Authenticity

Your leaders must learn the value of authenticity for executive leadership. Effective leadership and influence are born out of authenticity. No doubt you have been under a leader, as I have, who said one thing but did another. It is difficult for a leader to recover from this kind of misstep. When trust is eroded, it becomes impossible for others to believe in the vision and want to help bring that vision to fruition. We all witness such inauthenticity frequently. Political and organizational leaders who advocate for reduction of carbon emissions, for example, have been criticized for hosting big meetings complete with extreme consumption as participants fly in private jets to and from the venue. Additionally, during COVID, innumerable businesses laid off employees, including the transportation industry, and they struggle today to fill vacancies as people understandably hesitate to join organizations that made decisions that protected shareholders but proved devastating for employees.[2] Authenticity is a prerequisite for trust. And once it is undermined, it is difficult to recover. Having disparate standards in the C-suite that do not line up with the stated expectations of others in the organization is a recipe for crumbling culture and a declining organization. A critical lesson for C-suite–level leaders is to remember that team members will watch to be sure that you hold yourself to the same—or even more stringent—standards than those set for team members.

C-level leaders will need to work through critical financial challenges, raising capital sometimes at the expense of equity. These leaders must discern the financial and the partnership pieces and ensure they align with the organization's purpose and values. When emotions are running high because of budget shortfalls or unanticipated losses, it can be tempting to rush headlong into an ill-advised partnership that might "fix" a short-term issue but result in a much worse long-term problem. In these circumstances, I have been very intentional to recruit other leaders to share advice and provide feedback on the options, and I once backed out of a potential partnership as a result, saving myself and the organization from becoming entangled in a poorly structured, misaligned partnership.

Communication and Diplomacy

C-level leaders must also learn a level of diplomacy and, as is true for other leaders, a capacity for clear and thoughtful communication. These two things require wisdom and always go hand in hand. Diplomacy is important to maintain relationships and careless communication can set back progress or undermine it altogether. Poor diplomacy and bad communication are energy draining because they require tremendous amounts of time and correction to address the downstream effects. On the other hand, I believe it is possible for C-level leaders to build meaningful, lifelong partnerships with coworkers, and even partners outside the organization, when you have strong diplomacy and great communication.

As mentioned, I enjoy reading history and the ways that decision-making of late leaders resulted in enduring successes and a continuity of purpose. I work to glean the practical application, even when their context is distant from our own. I've always been particularly interested in the high level of diplomacy and excellent communication skills that George Washington exhibited during such a tenuous time for the emerging, fragile republic. To secure unanimous support for his presidential election surely was evidence of Washington's unusual capacity in this regard.[3]

Strong communication, as was outlined in the previous chapter for directors, does not happen in singular moments or in singular modes. It must be thoughtfully shared prior to, during, and following decisions, meetings, and/or events. Having a process for communication as it relates to change, initiatives, opportunities, or even celebrations is a strong rule of thumb. Additionally, diplomacy always includes inviting perspectives from others. C-level leaders should meet often individually with other leaders or team members to invite thoughts and perspectives. Keep in mind that it is more critical to listen than it is to speak in many of these meetings. However, ensure that those meetings include a strong recap of the vision to ensure it is understood.

Skilled diplomacy always balances posing good questions and interjecting appropriate information and commentary, ensuring that key voices are heard and considered. Following meetings, strong communication requires restating what was said and inviting clarification, if necessary. If meetings require an ultimate decision, again, ensure there is clear communication about the decision and the process taken to arrive at the decision. This care will help engender the buy-in and trust of other leaders and team members. Many leaders will enlist this kind of approach to build support and also to refine any elements based on the perspectives that were shared. Team members will be more likely to support a vision and a plan that they've had opportunity to advise or shape. Often, leaders skip steps or simply exercise their power and authority to make decisions that others had no opportunity to hear or weigh in on. It can be difficult to steer an organization as a C-level executive when you do not know how to exercise diplomacy and communicate consistently and clearly.

I think you'll agree that diplomacy seems in short supply these days within the political sector. Few seem to demonstrate the skills required to invite all perspectives and parties to the table to discuss complex problems with the intent of arriving at a decision that is best for more people. The best at diplomacy will lean into communication and dialogue with those who are adversaries and skillfully invite those who are allies, who might be even more skilled at framing the problem and potential solutions. I have created a decision framework that I use to help build coalitions with others who can be excellent advocates and team members for critical decisions and initiatives. I've found that, often, those other leaders can help boost the effectiveness of the plan and sometimes are best to help build the details of the communication framework of sharing information before, during, and/or after critical meetings.

Decision Framework

I decide who to include in the decision framework by considering the kind of influence and time needed to accomplish the new direction. I have a grid that I use where I write down names and roles. The grid includes various details about the colleagues and their level of involvement with the decision or process. Namely, I indicate their level of experience with the decision or initiative, the extent to which they will be affected, and the amount of responsibility they could have for implementation. I add names to each box and make sure different organizational levels are represented among each of these respective categories.

For many people, their spouse may not have a spot on the decision-making grid; however, since some of the decisions I make professionally could impact my family, due to how much time it may require of me or whether I'm making a significant financial decision, for example, I add my wife, Dana, to the grid. Besides my faith, my family is my second highest priority, and my decisions always work their way through the lens of my priorities. So, Dana likely will not have experience related to the specific work issue or decision, though it could have some effect on her. I add other names within the organization, of course, that have varying levels of experience and are likely to be affected by the decision at different levels.

After I do the mapping exercise, I begin to craft relevant questions for each of the people in these groups. Depending on who they are, what they have done, and the decision I am making, I meet with them, and then, after the meeting, I summarize what I heard as a follow-up. In recent years, one of the bigger decisions I have made in my life was to buy out a private equity position in my business. To have the freedom I needed to accomplish my vision for the company, I needed to be sole owner. As I was working through this decision, I created a decision framework and spoke with many people I'd included in my grid. I shared my vision, the strategic plan, financial considerations, team development needs, and some project-management details. I had people who could—and seemed willing to—help in all of these areas. They each, of course, brought different kinds and levels of knowledge and expertise. I had questions and conversations with each of these people to help inform the decision and process. I had conversations with them prior to, during, and after each meeting. I set up the conversation, hosted the meeting—during which we dove deeply into details—and again, followed up with each person to solidify what was next to begin work toward the desired outcome. In the middle of this process, the world was shut down due to the global COVID pandemic. The lending market was completely uncertain. I had many meetings in 2020 aimed at gaining approval for the transaction and worked hard to get the paperwork in place. It was at and through this time of uncertainty that I believe diplomacy and communication worked hand in hand, and while the mountain seemed very difficult to climb, we managed to close that deal at the end of June 2020, allowing me to become sole owner of the company.

Signal Timeline

2007–2008	2009–2010	2011–2012	2013–2014	2015–2016
Developed the current systems and security model	Ended 2009 with 10 franchises	Shareholders introduced	First vision trip	Brand became clearer
Defined franchise model & launched first franchise	Ended 2010 with 25 new franchises	Momentum slowed	Restructured within the organization to promote forward movement	Franchise group continued to develop
Ended 2008 with four franchises	Home office and financial system strained	Core values created	Revamped recruitment process to find the right partners	Company stabilized & matured
	Cashed in 401(k)/sold assets before December loan close			Team & self-development

2017–2018	2019–2020	2021–2023	2024–2025
Refined processes	Convention promoted growth	Decision made & process begins to rebrand the company	Adoption of new systems & infrastructure
Goals set	Focused on the vision for the company	Culture refined	Sales & development growth
Vision to become largest security company clarified	Role as leader of leaders	Officially launched brand refresh and completed in 2023	Global expansion
International growth	Franchise development process focused		
	Full company ownership achieved		

I also think that C-level leaders should aspire to build enduring organizations that outlast their leadership! They should aspire to identify and develop leaders who can carry the mission and vision forward in a way that transcends time, and even generations. To do this, it is incumbent upon the C-level leaders to craft a clear and compelling vision, reflect on that vision daily, and consistently make big and small decisions that help bring that vision to life. They must be able to communicate the vision individually and to groups of people so that they can understand it, whatever role they have. They should work to make decisions and lead with authenticity. They should exercise thoughtful diplomacy and communication.

As you develop potential leaders, look for those who demonstrate diplomacy and strong communications practices in the roles where they currently serve. Ensure that they use sound practices of asking good questions and including many perspectives. Teach them to practice communication before, during, and, especially, after meetings to be sure everyone is on the same page to help mitigate confusion. Consider using a framework to invite others' perspectives who can help inform decisions and be involved in implementation and/or advocacy.

While not every leader you identify and develop will end up in a C-level role, keep those skills and capacities top of mind as you begin to train and invest in someone for senior leadership. Be intentional about identifying the skills needed to build expertise and grow, and be sure that your leaders have chances to practice those skills. Be prepared for the privilege of promoting the development of someone whose leadership capacity exceeds your own. Yes, I did say that it is a privilege to help others grow and advance in their leadership journey! Don't bend to the temptation of self-preservation, because the very best test of any leader's capacity is their ability to spot and support other leaders. Multiplying leadership, as we will discuss soon, is the pathway to building sustainable, growing, enduring organizations. Checking ego at the door is critical to the work. Next, we'll consider some more tangible steps to launch the next generation of leaders into their roles. We will think more about how to develop leaders who will help the organization and its purpose to endure. You need to get ready to pass the torch.

SECTION FIVE

How Should You Develop Leaders?

I hope by now you are even more committed to developing leaders and that you see this work as critical to carrying forward a worthwhile purpose that endures. I hope that you believe it is critically important for your vision to transcend your own leadership. I hope that as you have read through each section, you have gained an ever-clearer picture of how you can help developing leaders practice the skills and capacities they need to serve and lead well.

You should now have a sense of why you should proactively identify and develop leaders, who you should consider, what capacities they need, and where within the organization's structure they can lead. Next, you'll think a bit more about how to develop them. This section will be a bit more tactical. It offers an approach that I've used to successfully help leaders learn to steer an organization through different stages of growth and an array of issues that could arise. You may find that you have naturally engaged some of these approaches as you've developed others, but hopefully you will gain a few additional development perspectives to leverage in the future. If you are ready to begin investing and developing a future next-generation leader, the following framework can steer how you approach the work: **demonstrate, delegate, motivate, and operate**.

CHAPTER 20

Demonstrate

As you develop new leaders, you should intentionally demonstrate the capacities and skills they need. While it is tempting to think about the most tangible elements of leadership roles, it is critical to demonstrate authenticity throughout the process. Ensure that you show your future leaders what it means to do what you say, follow through, and, as much as possible, live out your values, especially when no one is observing. Importantly, if leaders don't start figuring out ways to be authentic until they are in the C-suite, it will be tough to start doing it in the most visible role of all. So, model and practice it faithfully. Be real about the times when it feels tempting to be disingenuous and share what you do to maintain accountability to high standards in every conversation and decision.

Development Demands Self-Awareness

To demonstrate leadership qualities and capacities is a holistic endeavor for which you should prepare yourself. If you decide to do the work of developing others, self-assess whether you're ready for it. Find trusted colleagues and advisors to give you feedback about areas you might need to develop yourself to do the work well. It takes humility and work to do your part in developing others. Because your protégés are watching, you must be continually self-aware, demonstrate best practices, and put forward your best self in the process. You must commit to consistently operating at a high level so that you are demonstrating what you want them to emulate.

Demonstrating strong leadership is particularly hard when the proverbial weather is stormy, and it is easier when it's bright and sunny. Leadership capacity is best tested when things are difficult. This is when the most experienced leaders demonstrate the stability and hope required to steer others forward and show what it means to persevere. Again, however, authenticity is key. You will have difficult and challenging days, as everyone does. Being authentic as you demonstrate leadership skills means being honest and clear about the challenges and leading through them. It certainly does not mean that you sugarcoat or hide them. You do your colleagues a disservice if you fail to share the struggles, as well as the wins.

It is inspiring when this happens in sport. Highly experienced players, who have persevered and demonstrated elite skills that propel the team forward, are inspiring to other players who haven't yet had the same experience. I think of pitchers in baseball who take the mound in high-pressure games. I'm from Omaha, Nebraska, home of the College World Series. In 2021, the Mississippi State Bulldogs shut out Vanderbilt to win the series for the first time. Will Bednar was inspiring on the mound, pitching six shutout innings that helped clinch the game-three win in the finals and bring home the first-ever national title to Starkville. He was relieved by Landon Sims, who completed the game. Few pitchers have the experience of pitching a game for a national championship. The mindset and execution needed are intense and extreme. There are so many things to think about, and a young pitcher can learn to lead their team through the final inning by watching a tenured player do the work.

When I was in high school, I was a wrestler, and while I didn't have as much talent as other athletes, I experienced some success. My junior year, I advanced to the state finals. There was only one other wrestler on my team, a senior, who also qualified for the finals. That senior was undefeated. He had so many remarkable skills, as well as some matchday habits I tried to adopt. He not only won the state title, but he also was recruited to wrestle in college and went on to be an All-American and collegiate champion. After his competitive career was over, he pursued his love for the sport by coaching youth. I had the chance to reconnect with that teammate many years later, and we met up every so often. I once had a trip planned to Atlanta and invited him to come with me. He wanted to meet up with a specific wrestling coach and help facilitate their practice. My friend invited me to come along to watch! I was nervous since, well, it had been a whole lot of years since I'd been around the sport.

I realized quickly that my friend really knew his stuff. I had not been around the sport since high school, but clearly, my friend had continued to grow his knowledge and understanding of the sport and the methods for coaching the best techniques. During warm-up drills, he had them do a standing jump to help get fast-twitch muscles activated. The team was not putting their full effort into the drill, so he stopped the drill and decided to demonstrate it. He went up to the line, and I'm not kidding when I tell you it was astounding how far he leaped.

Those kids were in awe and completely focused on their special guest coach. The demonstrated excellence helped them understand that he was someone they could rely upon and learn from. While they had likely heard tips and techniques many times before, they were transformed and inspired by the coach who could demonstrate a high level of competency.

Demonstration works the same way when you are developing leaders within an organization. Simply describing and verbalizing tips and tricks is one way to share information, but they are easier to forget or ignore when they are not demonstrated. When people are shown, rather than just told, how to do or accomplish something, a respect for the person and the process grows. Words now have more weight. The instruction is not a tip but a point that is seen; it has breath and meaning. It moves from being an idea to being a way of working. It is no longer only academic; it is practical.

My story of my talented coach does not end there. At the first break, I told my friend how impressed I was with his jump. I pointed out that his ability to demonstrate success was a great coaching technique. He almost didn't remember what I was talking about, because that moment was just a brief one for him during the full coaching regimen and plan. He had already begun to focus on what to teach next based upon what he had observed and what he thought they needed to improve. He studied each of the athletes, considering their ages, size, and current skill sets. He wanted to help them make both big and subtle adjustments and assigned drills based on the data. He explained that the jump was part of a multistep warm-up routine that he teaches his wrestlers. He noted they also have classroom sessions on the mental aspects of the sport. These psychological training sessions help them focus in the moment and include video reviews to analyze and improve technique. They also study scenarios and when to implement moves, so they are prepared to initiate them and perform better in competitive settings.

Prepare, Perform, Review

Learners will be inspired by someone who competently demonstrates strong technique, but the point I do need to underscore here is the preparation of the coach. My friend knew that the jump just served as a technique to help secure the rapt attention of the athletes; it then opened the door to being able to demonstrate other sophisticated skills and drills that could be even more valuable for their future success. As a leader, prepare to demonstrate and follow this approach: prepare, perform, and review. To effectively demonstrate a skill, prepare for the right moment, the right skill, and the right execution and explanation of the skill. Then, of course, "perform" or demonstrate the skill—capably demonstrate it. It could be, as was the case with my coach friend, that demonstration is not the most critical aspect of the learning opportunity, but it will be part of the important whole. Then review the performance and the preparation. You need to share why the skill matters, but also review the effectiveness of the demonstration itself. Be ready to acknowledge to the leader you are developing the things that worked and things they might need to adjust in the future, depending upon the scenario. If you only focus on the performance—the actual demonstration—you won't be able to maximize the development opportunity, and it is not likely they can immediately turn that into a win. If you focus on preparing and practicing that skill and reviewing the performance with your future leader, there will be better opportunities for them to learn and perform it well later. You have the chance to teach the future leader that irrespective of how well a skill is demonstrated, continuous improvement is always the name of the game.

Consistent success only happens via preparing, performing, and reviewing the performance for improvement the next time. Remember to help your leader understand that preparation doesn't only include executing the specific task. Some work in leadership mandates active mental and emotional preparation as well. For example, having hard conversations about performance with a team member means that managers must prepare for the conversation by having all of the information and critical points ready to discuss, and it also means ensuring that you are prepared mentally to address questions, respond to emotions in a compassionate way, and find a time that each party is in a best frame of mind to have the hard conversation. This kind of task includes steps to prepare and execute, but it also involves self-assessment and physical preparation for various scenarios and needs that could arise. Making sure you are well rested to make sound judgments goes a long way for most any challenging task.

When people think about demonstrating leadership capacity for their protégés, most go straight to the performance itself. People are watching, and outcomes might be immediately evident, depending upon the circumstance or issue you are demonstrating. I once listened to a leadership development workshop leader who noted in his speech that even if we had heard him speak prior to that day, his intent was to customize the message for each audience, so he hoped learners would learn and take away something new. Other performers, such as musicians, tend to change their concerts or tours just a bit for each audience. As a leader, you should demonstrate that your performance can always be adjusted to be better the next time. Those little adjustments could make a big difference.

As you might have guessed, I really love watching championship sports. I really enjoy watching elite athletes compete and perform. You always see the best working hard to be even better and pushing even harder in the next inning, lap, or drive. Championship teams show up in championship games. While they may not have been holding back along the way, they often have another gear mentally, physically, and emotionally that they unlock when it is time. It is amazing when they are in the flow.

As you demonstrate leadership capacity, get to the point where you want to elevate your own "game." Don't settle for performance that is mediocre; teach your leaders that they, too, can always get better at their leadership performance. Create a highlight reel of leadership moments for those you are leading and challenge them to begin creating their own highlight reel!

Don't skip out on demonstrating how to review your performance. Model ways to stop and reflect. It is so easy to perform and move on and not think about it again until the next opportunity. Once a speech, a meeting, a conversation, a communication is done, you might feel exhausted and glad to have it checked off the list. But as you are demonstrating those things for your leaders, you should schedule the time to review and reflect. It's OK to take a pause and rest before hopping into the review, but make sure not to overlook it. There is humility in the process of reviewing performance that leaders must learn to embrace.

I tend to review my personal performance immediately following the activity or event, if possible, or at least later in the day. If it is a significant event or initiative, I might schedule periodic review opportunities to assess longer-term impact of the work or decisions. Based on what is learned from the review, new steps or adjustments can be made to the preparation next time. For example, I give a keynote speech at our annual convention. I prepare for many months—even over the entire year, honestly—building the stories and the content. Then the amount of attention paid to the address picks up considerably in the final weeks prior to the convention as I finalize what I am going to say.

As far as my company is concerned, that keynote is the biggest "performance" each year, as I review the current and project a future best state for the organization. I have built in the discipline of review for many years. However, as I have increasing demands on my time as the company grows, it has become increasingly more difficult to reserve the space for review. Rather than ditch the practice, I must be more intentional with scheduling it. I plan a break right after the keynote, for up to thirty minutes. I usually walk alone somewhere away from the event, or just head to my hotel room for a few minutes and think through or jot down what went well and what didn't. Then after the final event in the evening, I reflect more on what worked and what didn't that day. It's quiet, and the day's tasks are completed, so my mind is freer to process details. Following the convention, I head out on an annual vision trip to reflect on the big events, as well as the messages delivered to gauge the long-term implications of what was said and what listeners might have heard. One month post-event, I review it all again and work to assess whether any seeds of change have germinated because of the speech specifically, or the event generally.

As you develop other leaders, demonstrate what high-level success looks like. Model preparation, excellent performance, and review, so that—regardless of the skill or task you are demonstrating—your leaders will develop a posture of improvement. This isn't necessarily accomplished via quick tips, which will have a more limited shelf life, but is created via habits and a process that includes reflecting on what works and what impacts others. Teach your leaders that preparation is not just about the task and the steps, but also about mindset and preparing yourself in all domains—physically, mentally, and emotionally—to succeed. Prepare thoroughly, operate and perform at an elite level, but always review and be prepared to give more and add more to make leadership ventures most successful.

CHAPTER 21

Delegate

After you demonstrate important leadership principles and premises, you need to delegate a leadership opportunity to your aspiring leader so that they can begin to emulate what they've seen and heard. It could be that they need to see you demonstrate elements numerous times, but always look for best moments to delegate. Aspiring leaders need chances to share the stage and take responsibility. They need to practice.

Getting in the Game

Some strong leaders are not so strong at developing other leaders because they get stuck at this phase. They refuse to hand off tasks and rob the emerging leader of the chance to practice. Ultimately, without intentional delegation, the leader may experience early defeat if a moment comes when they must decide or respond, and they've not had the right opportunities to experience and practice. Again, leaning on a sports metaphor, this happens often when a starting quarterback takes every snap, and the backup never gets a chance to play a down in a game. If that reliable senior quarterback, who has never missed a single snap, is suddenly injured or ill, and the backup never saw playing time, it could be very difficult for that QB to enter the game and perform well under the lights. Coaches must balance the need to win games using their top talent with the need to develop the next emerging talent. If they don't, the whole team will be impacted by the leader's lack of experience, and it will be harder to execute well.

As a leader, it is tough to give up responsibility and delegate to a new leader. There might be important outcomes riding on the performance. And sometimes, if the task involves an external partner or customer, the task can be doubly difficult to surrender. But plan for that practice to give your emerging leader time, space, and grace to do the work. I recall a time many years ago when I went to the dentist. My family had gone to the same dentist for decades. Then, suddenly, a fresh, new dentist walked in after my cleaning. He had purchased the practice. The seasoned dentist observed the new colleague attentively, training him on various technical and business practices. He was preparing for that dentist to take over the practice within the next year.

Curious, as always, I began asking them questions. They talked about the transition and the ways the current owner would demonstrate various elements of the practice and begin to delegate those over time. Our dentist explained that he would be present for various meetings but delegate the leadership and decisions, coaching on things that might be improved or different depending on the circumstance. He said at some point he would no longer be present for meetings but would be available for some time in the office, in case help or advice was needed, but the work would be fully delegated at that point. The process was well thought out, and a useful framework put in place to demonstrate and then delegate different leadership principles and practices.

Plan on It

Delegation should be intentional and built on a timeline. Communicate expectations clearly when you are planning to delegate to your leaders. The transition and responsibility should be clear, and while it should be done with care, transitions should not be dragged out indefinitely.

As you delegate, be sure to recap the preparation and work that your leader has done. Make sure to follow through on any commitments you've made to your leader and remind them of helpful adjustments that were discovered during the review.

You may not always be able to control each circumstance as you delegate the leadership responsibilities to your future leader. Trust the process and preparation, be ready to support and steer, but also enjoy seeing their success and even their struggles, as those often are the best opportunities for leaders to learn and grow.

Phone calls and virtual meetings are common activities I use in our business to begin delegations to leaders I'm developing. If we're talking to a potential customer, for example, we can partner to develop the agenda ahead of time. I might join the call, but I let the new leader facilitate. It is easy to review and debrief the call and then make suggestions for the future. Sometimes, I can coach the new leader on the call around points to cover or adjustments to make, but I minimize real-time input, so the leader can remain focused on the customer and objectives at hand. I can also decide which calls to help new leaders be a part of, starting with those that are lower stakes and moving to more intense calls that require real-time, highly consequential decision-making.

Once you've had a chance to observe your emerging leader, it's important to know when to exit the proverbial playing field to let the emerging leader lead. You might watch on the sidelines and provide coaching, especially if asked, later. Educators understand the importance of letting their students try, occasionally fail, and try again. Be sure that you've created an environment that values trying and turns failure into learning opportunities. You can crush a person's growth and development if you do not extend the grace needed to make changes the next time.

Identify the places and spaces where it makes sense in your organization to let an emerging leader test their wings. You should be available, observing and ready to nudge, if a catastrophic failure is of enormous consequence, but resist the urge to correct too much, particularly if the failure is indeed fixable. Document and be sure that you delegate only those things you've clearly set expectations for and which you've been able to demonstrate. And always be sure to note strengths in action. As you delegate, always encourage. This is critical so that they become accustomed to leaning on their strengths, while they also learn to delegate to promising leaders who might have areas of expertise and strength that they do not.[1] Encourage the learner to practice the preparation, the performance, and the review pieces of the work. The more they go through that process for a practice or principle, the greater their confidence and capacity as a leader will be.

Support and Encourage

Again, be available to provide support as needed. Once they practice, the need for support will taper off, but don't abandon them just because they have been successful. Your leader might be ready for new learning, and you might feel relief that some work has been successfully transitioned. However, you don't want insecurity or nerves to seep in. If you want to know how much your leader would like to touch base, try asking them! You should focus on their growth, so they don't revert to bad habits and tendencies, and instead, again, look for the habit of continuous improvement and striving for excellence.

I have great respect for Dr. Tom Osborne, the legendary Nebraska Cornhuskers football coach for twenty-five years. He led the team to three national championships in the 1990s. Following the 1997 championship, he retired and his assistant coach took the reins. He had modeled strong leadership and values for his colleagues and athletes as a coach and has modeled those same values since his retirement. In his book, *More Than Winning*, Coach Osborne gave recognition to his coaching staff, noting, "Also meriting appreciation are my fellow coaches at Nebraska, who have done so much to make our program what it is." John E. Roberts, who partnered in producing the book, noted, "[Coach Osborne] is a humble servant. He's also honest—uncompromisingly honest . . . At a time when characters receive more press than character, this man's story is a welcome change." Coach Osborne's approach to leading and coaching is consistent, modeling servanthood and an expectation of doing and being good. He remains remarkably reserved in the public eye about the work of other coaches, but he has remained engaged and supportive. He and his wife, Nancy, started a school-based youth mentoring organization, TeamMates Mentoring, many years ago, and it has made a positive impact across the region. Coach Osborne has remained humble and available to the nonprofit he founded, the university, the football program, and the community at large in the many years since his retirement.[2]

Find a Cadence

As you delegate work and opportunities to your new leaders, be supportive, humble, and available. Begin by setting up a cadence of check-in meetings over time, depending upon what your emerging leader needs and the complexity of the tasks or role. Generally, if you opt to develop a leader, you may change that cadence over time, depending, again, upon how complex their work is and their need for development. Invite the leader to ask questions and get a sense of the advice they need. Don't assume and don't presume unless you've observed performance firsthand. Trust your new leaders. They will be grateful for that trust. Ultimately, new leaders need opportunity, some coaching, and, most of all, encouragement and support.

It can be hard to delegate. But as you delegate, you can experience the satisfaction of seeing a new leader emerge. Let the leader have a chance to lead, observe and follow up with them, and be available to listen and encourage. Be ready to celebrate when someone you develop takes the reins successfully. It's the highest calling of a leader to help others realize their potential.

CHAPTER 22

Motivate

To motivate others is to understand the power of words, to know what people need, and to influence effort and work to help drive desired outcomes. It is important for people to find innate motivation in their work and to be able to pursue their purpose and do more of what they do best. But often, leaders need to help others understand the purpose and vision and rally support for it.

Teach your leader to motivate others and use their influence to build a positive culture that drives action and follow-through. These are the conditions that are healthiest for success to occur. You want the leaders you develop to understand and recognize that their words and actions affect people, and you want them to be able to anticipate those effects. As they find ways to motivate, you want them to be able to analyze their words and meanings. Leaders sometimes fail to think about the specifics of communication that can support motivating and positive messages, such as cadence, voice inflection, body language, and, of course, crafting content that includes the right combination of stories and information. Being able to motivate others can help drive efficient and effective leadership. Help your leaders learn to motivate, and they will have more capacity to facilitate positive outcomes and fulfill the vision and purpose.

Communicate to Motivate

As leaders grow, they can take on additional responsibilities, so it is critical to help them build effective communication skills. The more sophisticated leaders are at leveraging various kinds of communications platforms and messaging, the more effectively they can build relationships and help steer the direction for the teams and the organization overall.

Strong communicators, first, speak truth. They do not try to deceive their audience. Again, leaders are authentic and practice transparency as a rule. Timing is critical when delivering difficult news, and the way difficult news is shared is, of course, extremely important. But having a posture that is authentic, and messaging that is clear and unambiguous, is important for leaders to be able to maintain trust and motivate others to work toward shared and desired outcomes.

Regrettably, there are countless examples dedicated to those who may have motivated others for a time but did so with devious and greedy intent. These individuals literally and figuratively rob others of peace and prosperity for their own gain. Leaders are tasked with the responsibility of creating the best environment that will promote the well-being of those in their care, while accomplishing the vision of the organization so that it can endure to the benefit of future generations!

Leaders who fail to share truth and who fail to understand the needs of listeners will miss their opportunity to motivate and inspire. Leaders often have the joy of sharing good news and celebrating successes in their messaging, but also must share challenges and difficult hurdles. Doing each of these things in a way that motivates rather than discourages takes preparation, practice, and, again, careful review of the outcomes and a commitment to learning from communications flubs.

Empathy Is Inspiring

Motivating others toward positive outcomes requires empathy, compassion, and focus on their needs and perspectives. It also requires indefatigable passion and promotion of the vision and hope for outcomes. No one will be excited on behalf of the leader. Excitement and passion are caught, but for people to feel it, leaders must genuinely possess it and share it. If the leader is unsure about the outcome they hope to achieve, rest assured, their teams won't be able to untangle it from their message. Passion must accompany empathy. Excitement cannot trump care. Help your leaders learn to show their care for the teams who are most impacted by changes and initiatives. Passion must be apparent, and they need to show their own commitment to those outcomes. That passion for the vision should be matched by the care for team members. If either of these are neglected, a leader may fall short in delivering the motivating message they intended to deliver.

Most of us love inspirational movies that tell stories of underdogs who keep fighting and beat all odds. The passion that drives and pushes them forward causes us to reflect on our own journey and experiences and ways we can overcome obstacles. The movie *Rudy* is such a classic in the space. The movie tells the story of "Rudy" Rudiger, who was a walk-on football player for the Notre Dame Fighting Irish. He was a small fellow, with little likelihood of ever starting a game, but he was a relentlessly hard worker, who refused to let the fact that he was undersized for a D1 powerhouse football team prevent him from achieving his dream to make the team. He took a beating in practices time and again, but his passion to play for the Fighting Irish persisted despite the pain. Spoiler alert! In the end, he earns his spot and gets his moment in the sun, accomplishing his dream. The team and the fans cheer because they share his love and passion for the storied program. Rudy's passion won over the crowd. Rudy wasn't the best player with the most potential, but he motivated and influenced those around him, because his passion was infectious. This is the power of passion to positively motivate others to achieve the best outcomes.

When we look for an empathetic leader who can motivate others, Oprah Winfrey is a strong example. For decades, she pulled on America's heartstrings on her TV show, inviting guests who were fighting difficult circumstances and iconic entertainers who shared their personal and professional stories. Oprah was an empathetic connector of people. Emotion for a purpose was a mainstay of her storytelling. She weaved together the stories of her guests with the experiences of her audience. People could feel that someone else felt with them. Her gift giving was an effective and tangible way to show care for her audience members. She was unique in her capacity to build passion and steer sentiment.

Strong leaders know how to motivate by exhibiting both passion and empathy. Help your leaders learn to communicate with the intent to motivate and galvanize their teams around shared goals and outcomes. The best leaders are focused on the outcomes that are good for the entire team or organization; they are not only focused on what can be gained for themselves. The ability to rally the team around outcomes that are mutually beneficial and around a vision that is larger than oneself is special. While some people will be more naturally able to do this,

Motivate

every leader can learn some skills to be more motivating and effective in their communication.

If a leader is most concerned about themselves, the team will see it, and it will be difficult to gain traction long term as an influencer. But when a leader intends to motivate toward outcomes that are positive for both the individual and the organization, it can be energizing.

It seems more common today to have purpose-driven organizations advertise their focus on the social good. A good example of this is TOMS® shoes. They built the business brand on a one-for-one model, giving away one pair of shoes to someone in need for each pair that is sold.[1] They now advertise that they give away one-third of their profits to various causes. One of their differentiators is their focus on doing good in the world. Their passion and empathy are closely paired and have motivated customers globally to engage with them. Their altruistic global approach helped to put their brand on the map.

Strong leaders can motivate others for good. As you develop leaders, demonstrate and coach them on how to motivate others around what matters most for everyone. Encourage them to tap into their passion for the purpose and vision of the future, as well as their empathy for people. Passionate, empathetic leaders are motivating leaders, and these leaders can positively steer and sustain an organization's future for years to come.

CHAPTER 23

Operate

Finally, to help leaders grow, you need to help them learn to operate at a high level. If leaders have the training, skills, and opportunity, but do not maximize those opportunities to fine-tune their skills in different scenarios and circumstances, their potential will not be fully realized as a leader. It is akin to a high-powered, well-designed sports car that sits safely on display in a garage but is never tested on the road. Leaders must learn to operate within their organization's system(s). They need to practice and test their skills in a variety of scenarios, departments, and projects at the organization.

Go, Listen, Correct, Direct

For leaders to operate at a high level, teach them to go and listen to their teams. Then, teach them to correct and direct, if needed. The order is important. Someone who never listens will have a tough time correcting and directing, because the relationship is likely not there. People learn best from people they know care about them. Again, I personally lean on the example of Jesus's leadership as He spent decades preparing for His earthly ministry, and then three years of ministry that changed the course of history. Jesus went where people were. He went where the need was, asked key questions, listened, then offered correction and clear direction, whether He was meeting with the woman at the well and listening to her story (John 4) or a rich young ruler (Matthew 19). This will help guide the framework for your leaders.

First, as they learn to lead at work, leaders should understand the power of presence. Go. Be with people to understand their work, their decisions, and the choices that they are making each day. Like the director of our house-building project in Ecuador demonstrated, it is imperative that leaders spend some time being present with their teams to understand their challenges and to celebrate their big and small wins. There is power in being present. This is true for every area of our lives. When a friend is hospitalized, another is getting married, someone is graduating, or a sudden memorial service is planned, there is enormous meaning and power in presence. To go and be present during the most significant transition moments in our lives is very meaningful. Similarly, to operate best, it is important that leaders understand the power of going. Be sure to demonstrate for your leaders what it means to go and be present. Show the contexts and spaces where it is important to go—this could be a personal or work context. People remember the effort made to go and be present.

I've spent much of my career in a sales capacity, and I am keenly aware of the value of asking good questions. Since it is easier for people to believe what they themselves say, rather than what others say, asking questions is paramount to trust building. Skilled salespeople want others to think and decide on their own about the value of the product or service. The salesperson facilitates the process primarily by asking good questions, listening, and being prepared to respond. Early in my career, I used to skip the step of asking and listening, and thought I'd just jump right in to directing. I learned, though, that if I invested in the conversation—and the person—by listening better to their needs and steering their understanding and perceptions of the product, that I had a better opportunity to connect and make the sale. The sale became about meeting the need more than selling the product.

There are times when it is not enough to just go and be present. You must absolutely help leaders learn the powerful skill of asking and listening. It is such an underutilized and underappreciated skill. Especially if your leaders are natural communicators, it could be difficult for them to practice listening. Filling airtime with our own words can be a compulsion to fight for many of us—me included, admittedly! The inclination to talk instead of listen is often strong, especially in hard or difficult conversations. But in significant moments, transition times, and even everyday happenings, listening should replace talking. Sometimes our own words fall flat and don't have the intended impact if the leader has not first listened—and as they say, understanding comes from listening rather than responding. Asking good questions is one way to demonstrate how to listen. Questions, of course, invite responses, and leaders can learn to pause and listen. Help them learn to ask questions before offering advice. Connections are built through listening. It centers on the other person rather than your own agenda. It is something all leaders need to learn, and it is harder for some than others. Demonstrate this for the leaders you develop.

Listening frees people to just be themselves, and you learn about their needs. At work, the primary job of leaders is to help meet workplace needs so that individuals and teams can perform at their best.

Some managers and leaders are afraid to ask questions and listen because they fear they can't respond in the way their teams want or need. But not listening is a sure way to isolate the team and create distance. Even if you are not able to immediately change the circumstance or need, going and listening, together, provides a powerful message that you care and want to connect. I also believe that creative ways to steer or correct a situation are illuminated in the act of listening. Let's turn to correction next.

Listening connects leaders with individuals and with teams, but correction and direction have the capacity to be transformative. The best leaders are transformative. Leaders who learn to operate at a high level should be able to help transform people, workplaces, and cultures, providing the best opportunity for long-term, sustainable success for people and the organization. While it is important to first connect with people via going and listening, it's important to take the next step to make progress. Keep the future in mind as you consider the next layer of leadership, which is to correct, when and if needed.

Transformation happens with correction and direction. Transformative experiences happen when something changes and becomes something much more valuable and enduring. Correction might need to happen with respect to the individual's work performance. Correction is about what they should change or stop doing. And, importantly, direction is about what to start doing instead. I recommend always including both. Note, it could also be that the circumstances, environment, working relationships, or even the space and materials must change to make progress.

Personally, my wife, Dana, graciously corrected some of the ways I approached our children. She demonstrated how to provide choices and how to ask questions and listen to their answers—and to do that at eye level. As they got older, I began to coach and direct when they needed

Operate

advice and support. These changes have had such a positive impact on my connection and influence with my kids, my family, and our relationships in the long term. Informed by her expertise in education and child development, Dana helped by demonstrating and correcting some of my approaches, and it was transforming for me.

This kind of transformative approach is important for leaders to be able to operate at their best. You want to develop leaders—not for the moment, a temporary event, or a project—who have positive influence and can lead for a lifetime in any circumstance. To operate this way effectively, help your leaders learn to go, listen, correct, and direct, as needed. Demonstrate this framework for your leaders, putting it into practice within your personal and your professional life to be consistent and authentic. Your leaders will learn to appropriate these steps, operate at a higher level, and build transformative, growing teams!

SECTION SIX

Leadership That Lasts

Finally, let's think about what your current and future leaders need to facilitate ongoing, exponential growth in individuals and your organization. To have a vision that becomes reality and a purpose that endures for many generations, you must develop leaders who are able and willing to **create** new things, can learn to **regulate**, are prepared to **accelerate** growth, can assess the **future state**, and set up leadership relationships in **triplicate**.

CHAPTER 24

Create

For organizations to endure, they must learn to create something new. American theologian Leonard Sweet is credited with saying, "Change is life. Stagnation is death. If you don't change, you die. It's that simple. It's that scary." Humans must create to remain relevant and responsive to a dynamic environment. They must change in response to it. They must carefully consider core values and identify what should stay the same and what must change as time passes. Leaders and organizations that choose not to create something new will ultimately fail, because change is the only truly reliable thing. Leaders must create with the purpose of the organization in mind, extending the work and impact of the organization into a future that cannot ever be fully known or anticipated. It is both the challenge and the reward of leading people and organizations—to anticipate the future and to create new things to meet that uncertain future.

See the Needs

I think UPS has been successful at this over the years. Many are familiar with the UPS delivery company, with its brown trucks and reliable drivers who deliver packages, but that is not how the company started. Founded in 1907, entrepreneurs Claude Ryan and Jim Casey wanted to build a business and serve people. They first opened a bicycle repair and parts shop but realized automobile use was skyrocketing, threatening their business. They were at a crossroads and needed to adapt or risk losing their business. As they analyzed their business and its strong points, delivering parts to their customers was a unique and successful element to their business.

Occasionally, as they did their work, merchants or store owners asked them to deliver goods for them to other parts of town. They paid them for their trouble. The business leaders realized there was a lucrative opportunity in delivery work. They intentionally added a delivery service to their business repertoire, charging based on the item and the time and distance they needed to travel. The company now known as UPS was born. The leaders were responsive to the shifting market and created a new line of business that enabled them to endure but was still true to their core purpose of serving customers.[1]

Leaders must look for ways to create new opportunities when change is clearly on the horizon, and even sometimes when things are simply stable. The purpose of the organization can remain the common thread that drives creativity. I think of creativity as imagining new and original ideas to produce or improve something that changes how we live, learn, or work. Passionate and motivated leaders are sometimes driven to create, but creating for its own sake is not the point. There are countless cautionary tales of new creations that alienated a customer base, and damage control was required to earn back that business. Not all new ideas and creations are a resounding success, and hindsight is, of course, always much clearer than our foresight in those instances.

Coca-Cola, for example, decided to jimmy with their original recipe and launched "New Coke" in the 1980s. In a misguided effort to make it sweeter, they launched the redesigned product. It was, of course, a failure.[2] They lost credibility with their customers, and the public pushback was intense. The product was canceled, and the original "Coca-Cola Classic" retook its rightful place as their representative brand.

In bringing back the original Coke, the brand was refreshed in people's minds, and they remembered why they liked it! Coca-Cola also opted to expand their product offerings, introducing new drinks. The company introduced new drinks after field-testing what worked, following trends, listening to their customers, but always keeping their flagship offering unchanged. They were experiencing loss in market share, which drove the idea to recreate the original Coke. They have since, however, ventured into non-carbonated drinks and bottled water and innovated with their "Zero" lines to build their brand and maintain customers as palates and dietary interests continue to shift. Creating and recreating involves testing, learning, and trying again, as needed, to build and sustain growth and momentum over time.

Similarly, McDonald's wanted to expand its business and was looking to update its menu. They updated the menu to include more options, but many had largely failed. The company needed to stay close to its core value proposition of providing fast, reasonably priced food. Newly introduced items sometimes took longer to prepare and weren't what customers wanted. McDonald's continued to adjust and, in 1971, California franchisee Herb Petersen introduced the industry's first on-the-go breakfast sandwich—the Egg McMuffin, which has been one of the most successful items on the company's menu. It was offered nationally by 1975.[3] This item expanded their service from lunch and dinner to include early morning breakfast. To date, no other fast-food chain competes with McDonald's in breakfast volume. It is a lesson in having humility to change course, review what went wrong, and be willing to take a new approach and direction.

Study, Test, Offer, Expand

Help your leaders by offering a framework to determine whether it is time to create something new to move the organization forward. McDonald's roughly had this approach in entering the breakfast market. They studied and market tested the Egg McMuffin, then expanded it to all stores once it was successful.

First, learn to study what the market needs or wants and then test what might work. Don't create something that clearly won't work in the market. If you create a new thing internally with little to no understanding of what the market wants or needs, you will not be able to know which variables are critical to success. When I started Signal, the market needed options for security patrol services (see Signal Timeline in Chapter 19, page 147). The franchise model was not yet firmly established in this business arena. We studied what might work and ways to set up the franchises. Sometimes it is difficult to secure the data you need to decide on a new thing. But you should encourage your leaders to refuse to design and create without research. To test our model, we sold just a few franchises. Several of those franchises are still in business today. It was extremely valuable to learn what customers needed and what franchise owners required to be successful. I owned a franchise myself out of the gate. It was invaluable to test the processes and systems needed for scheduling, efficiently running routes, and handling personnel needs, as well as other business processes.

Create

Not every new idea will work, and sometimes what works will surprise you. This is true of chicken wings! My grandfather and ancestors were farmers. My dad told me that chicken wings were originally used as pig food. They really didn't think that chicken wings would sell, and while they certainly would not go to waste for those who raised chickens, at least from my grandfather's perspective, the only real purpose was feeding them to pigs. In Buffalo, New York, a restaurant decided to test frying the wings and selling them with a sauce. There are some twists and turns to the story and some debate about who ought to receive credit for selling them first, but we all know there's now a big market for chicken wings and several stores that sell them. Not only do restaurants now offer buffalo (or other) chicken wings on their menus, but whole brands have also been built and expanded to many corners of the country around chicken wings.[4]

After testing confirms the need for the idea or product you want to create, you need to then offer the product or service. It is important to systematically offer the product or service in a focused and defined way to allow additional data and information to inform the expanded rollout. This was done in big ways as we structured our franchise security service offerings. After offering the patrol service in several franchises, we learned a great deal more before initiating and expanding widely. Encourage your leaders not to miss the step of offering the newly created product or service prior to expanding it broadly in your area or market. If you jump right into expanding the offering, it's possible to miss a detail that could blunt the returns you're hoping for.

Wendy's has always prided itself on fresh, never frozen hamburgers. As the meat aged, they knew that they needed to sell it before it spoiled, but they were committed to not freezing the meat, and they didn't want to throw it out before its shelf life expired. One leader had the idea to offer chili, using hamburger meat. This, and other special menu items, had some success. The consumers gave feedback on the item, they adjusted the offering, and then finally, Wendy's built the item into their brand and marketing. After that, they were ready to expand the item into all stores.[5]

Once Wendy's could reference the right market information and data to inform their pricing and packaging, they were ready to expand. They could successfully offer chili at all their stores, putting an ad campaign behind it. It's a consistent offering for them that was good for managing the business and met a consumer preference.

Leaders will need to learn to create new lanes of business or initiatives that work. As you develop new leaders in your organization, help them avoid mistakes that might lead the business in the wrong direction and alienate hard-earned followers and customers. Encourage them to think through the following framework as they create and initiate new ideas, products, and/or services: study, test, offer, and expand. It is a general framework with utility in most industries, from fast food to security services. You can help a leader dramatically increase their chances for success, as they understand the value in creating new things, but doing so in a way that keeps the organization's purpose and vision in mind and ensuring they follow a workable process to test the idea. Next, help your leaders understand what it means to regulate.

CHAPTER 25

Regulate

To regulate has many connotations, and I recognize they are not all positive! Regulation is a critical part of any organization's work and influences its capacity to succeed. At its best, external regulation helps support fairness, safety, and order, while protecting freedom to make choices. It allows for the fair expansion of work and opportunity. Regulation over time in this country has yielded more freedom and fairness, but, of course, history is also replete with examples of regulation riddled with a lack of fairness and oppressiveness. It is not the intent of this chapter to track those innumerable lessons, but I suggest you encourage your leaders to review and understand their role. Leaders need to have a lens through which to understand both internal and external regulation and policymaking and their role in leadership and impact on their organization. They need to recognize whenever regulation fails to promote freedom, fairness, or safety.

People need order and protection to best work and perform. Regulation can bring order and the stability needed for people and the organization to flourish. Regulation and policymaking work best when they balance and maintain order and protect fairness and freedom.

Self-Regulate

Perhaps it goes without saying, but I will say it anyway! Leaders must practice self-regulation. Self-regulation—controlling one's emotions and behavior—is supported by practicing authenticity and accountability. Effective leaders are disciplined, do what they say they will do, and abide by the values and policies the organization has established.

Followers need trust, compassion, stability, and hope.[1] One way to promote these is for leaders to be self-aware and able to self-regulate. In short, a positive culture is difficult to establish when leaders are inconsistent and unpredictable themselves. Leaders must be able to prioritize the needs and emotions of others.

High-operating leaders understand, too, that regulation can help avoid the temptation of working for self-gain rather than working and serving to support others. A proficient leader will always be learning and growing, but once they move from needing active development, they should still have ongoing accountability. Accountability helps leaders stay on track and avoid the pitfalls in decision-making that could result in downfalls that impact many. Regulation brings both order and accountability, which must remain a part of the way that every strong leader operates.

Navigate Intentionally

There are some sectors that are heavily regulated, and, again, it goes without saying that leaders are responsible for abiding by those regulations and ensuring adequate resources are allocated so the organization abides by them. In our company's space, we are a national, increasingly global, security franchising firm, and every state has different licensing requirements and regulations that franchise owners must know. Being proactive to support new franchisees and their businesses, while modeling how to incorporate those into the business set up process, is key to helping them be successful. Sometimes patience is just part of the equation. Once the franchise has been established on a solid foundation and followed required steps, they will ultimately experience less barriers to growth and expansion.

Maintain Order, Freedom, and Fairness

Regulation for any institution informs and influences how it grows. At best, it keeps fairness, safety, and freedom in balance to support expansion and growth. As you help your leaders figure out how to set policy and regulate the workplace or other aspects of the organization, make sure to also help them understand the freedoms that are valued in your workplace. Decide whether it is the freedom to choose what time to work, to speak your mind, to dress, to choose your space—whatever it is—then determine what order is required to make progress. Then teach your developing leaders what variables to consider as you choose to expand your organization and ways that it will impact all concerned parties. Be committed to fairness and freedom, while maintaining order. Consider what freedoms you can never lose, and what order is needed. Then figure out how and where the organization can work and expand.

I personally feel particularly strongly about freedom of speech. While there is never a mandate to listen, everyone should have their voice heard. But the only way it works is if there is also some regulation. With some order in place, everyone has space and time to be heard.

To say it more succinctly, if no one listens, freedom of speech is futile, with no utility. In short, it is necessary to regulate. There is freedom to communicate, as well as an expectation to regulate—externally and internally—to protect and honor that freedom for all.

Leaders should aim for establishing order and stability in the organization and balance that with the need to allow freedoms that the organization values, where possible. As you initiate policies or workplace norms, make sure that employees, customers, and others who intersect with your organization understand those values and that they are guarded with your policies and practiced with trust. People should always know what choices they have and where there is freedom to choose. Everyone should have freedom to express themselves and fulfill their job, while maintaining an order that ensures that same opportunity for everyone. It can be tough to know when and how to make and enforce policies around things like hybrid work environments, dress codes, or PTO, but help your leaders know that it is possible to over- and underregulate.

Do No Harm

Seasoned leaders must maintain a strong commitment to work legally and ethically and, when possible, approach other elements of workplace practices with fairness and order. Again, help leaders commit to organizational growth that does no harm and does so fairly. Encourage them to actively seek and analyze different variables and ways that expansion will impact current and future employees and influence the customers and the business overall. Help your leaders understand that expanding a business causes stress on individuals, resources, and even the market. To expand while keeping fairness foremost in our minds requires intentionality and a fresh lens. If you are opening a new store, another branch, or selling a new franchise in a new region, or simply adding another meeting with a team member to execute your project, be sure to see the actions through the lens of fairness. Ensure that everyone has an opportunity to contribute and perform and do their best. Be aware of the ways that resources and support are apportioned and how that apportionment is perceived. There may indeed be policies that regulate and dictate some of the business and finance decisions that a leader must make. Be transparent and realize not everyone may understand that. Ensure that your leaders know what they need to know, so they don't get themselves or the organization in trouble. Be sure that leaders are aware of their responsibility to communicate the organization's ideals. They need to keep others *and* themselves accountable to work in ways that are both fair and ethical.

Leaders must abide by the regulations and expectations that are established to guard the culture and ensure that fairness and order are upheld. They are responsible to steward the process of establishing, knowing, and upholding appropriate regulation that fosters both freedom and fairness, promoting the long-term stability of the organization.

CHAPTER 26

Accelerate

Next, highly effective leaders help to accelerate the healthy growth of their organization. Many organizations will experience a period of rapid acceleration. If the organization does not experience this, complacency can soon lead to decline. It is an important part of healthy organizations with significant purpose and vision. Effective leaders need to be able to anticipate and facilitate the opportunity to accelerate gains and growth. These are some of the most fun and exciting times in an organization's history. Acceleration is an increasing rate of velocity. These are the times during an organization's growth that are not only incremental or systematic growth times but moments when growth is in overdrive and moving ahead rapidly.

A time of acceleration might include a big win, a new project successfully launching, expanding locations, or a rapid influx of revenue through some other means. I've also found that these times of rapid acceleration have a layer of risk and potential for failure as well. So, it is important for leaders to be ready to make the requisite decisions that enable the growth rather than hinder it. These are tough things to teach a new leader. Experience is, of course, a vital component to leading through such a time. As you develop leaders, be particularly aware of when you need to invite them to observe and participate in the thought processes and operations that underlie a time of accelerated growth and expansion.

Mechanically, if a vehicle accelerates beyond its capacity, it can break apart. If there is even just one part or component not up to par with the rest of the structure, it might still break apart. Organizations have many parts to the whole, and when all elements are prepared for growth, it can be exciting, but that readiness must be designed.

When I turned sixteen, it was time for me to purchase my first car. My dad asked me to get the newspaper to look for cars for sale. (Yes, at that time we still looked up ads in the paper.) It won't shock you to know that I wanted a "Vette." What teenager wouldn't be excited by the look and speed of such a fantastic vehicle? I frankly didn't care about having lots of seats for passengers. I only needed to drive myself to school and work every day. My dad responded in typical dad fashion and questioned me and my decision-making. He declared there was no way I'd be able to afford such a vehicle, nor was I an experienced enough driver and car owner to have such a car. In the end, at sixteen years of age, I become the proud owner of my first "Vette"—a Chevy Chevette, that is. This little gem was a bestseller for a few years in the late '70s and '80s, but you might not know about this classic. It was a small, affordable car, used by commuters. What it lacked in luxury, it made up for in cost-effectiveness and practicality.

While I didn't get my dream Corvette to practice high-speed turns and acceleration on the road, I could at least say, "I drive a Vette!" Ha!

And while my car was not engineered for performance like a Corvette is, that didn't keep me from trying to push it to perform like one. I don't recommend that teens try this at home, of course, but every time I got behind the wheel, I tested the performance limits of that car. I would break too hard, slam on the gas, and take turns a bit too fast. I tested the limits of acceleration, trying to reach the speed limit of the road quickly. For the first couple of months that I had my new "Vette," the car responded just fine, and I was adjusting and figuring out what it could do. However, after about six months, I was driving it and noticed smoke coming from the engine. I decided the best course of action was to disregard it—yikes. I know. It didn't happen all the time, so I reasoned it was probably steam. Then, a week or two after I first noticed the smoke, the car had absolutely no power. I was stumped. I finally worked up the courage to admit to my dad that there was something wrong with my car. Because I was driving the car too hard, the line that provided coolant to the engine had burst, and it was leaking fluid. Since I did not adjust or repair the line, all the fluid was gone. The engine overheated, and one of the four cylinders cracked. My beloved Vette was no more.

I didn't have a good handle on the limitations and capabilities of my car, so I literally drove it into the ground. Similarly, leaders who are not aware of the capacities of their organization may not have a good sense of when to push for growth and when to slow and let infrastructure and capacity catch up and stabilize. High-functioning leaders learn to gauge signs across all areas of the organization to determine when it is time to move ahead and expand or introduce new products or initiatives. When leaders accelerate and ignore signs that the organization has exceeded its current capacity, they can run into painful results, which might include losing valuable staff members, dated and overtaxed systems or technology, or strained resources and budgets, which can harm the organization and its potential future. There are many examples of businesses that went awry because their leaders accelerated beyond what the organization could rightly manage. It never ends well. Poor decisions and poor timing can end a fun run for organizations, and it is terribly humbling to face those affected.

Teach your leaders that there is a balance between a time of accelerated growth and patience and wisdom to ensure the organization is prepared. It is imperative to remember and practice each of the leadership capacities—revisit the vision, plan strategically, maintain strong financial management, and manage projects well. It is much wiser to accelerate growth intentionally than it is to come back from the point of disaster when the decisions and path wreck the organization.

Hush Puppies is one brand that experienced an amazing resurgence in popularity and sales. The company was built in the mid-twentieth century on providing comfortable, casual shoes. Then in the '90s, the brand experienced a sudden acceleration in growth. They became popular in New York clubs, celebrities began to wear them, and the company quadrupled year-over-year sales by the mid-'90s.[1]

An accelerated growth phase is exciting but requires tremendous intensity and focus. Leaders cannot be distracted and can't let up. A framework your leaders can use to manage through a period of acceleration includes carefully monitoring communication, inspecting and analyzing supply lines, and preparing for reinforcements.

Monitor Communication

Ensure your leaders know that during accelerated growth and expansion they need to carefully monitor communication. Beware of communication that only shares positive data and stories but fails to include challenging and hard information. Help leaders look for what is not said as much as what is. Ask hard questions about what data and information are missing or what scenarios are influencing the data. Leaders must learn to be critical—not cynical, but critical. If all that leaders hear and learn is positive information, it could be there are biases at play, and team members must be challenged to find indicators that they may be missing. I neglected to give my dad a key piece of information in time to save my Vette: namely, that the car was not being as responsive. Then there was smoke, but I didn't say anything then, either. I waited until the engine was already busted. Teach your leaders to heed all cautionary data.

Leaders must learn to listen for those things that are not said and think critically about potential scenarios that have not yet been considered so that the team can proactively prepare for them. Additionally, ensure that leaders ask questions and invite feedback from people at all levels across the organization so that different perspectives on progress are shared. Ensure that the information you monitor is not only from directors, but also includes feedback from associates and managers and includes project details and stories. Senior and executive leaders should share information about finances, budget, resources, and team dynamics. Teach your leaders to plan for the time and energy to monitor communications and gather input.

Inspect Supply Lines

Teach your leaders that during accelerated growth times, not only must they carefully monitor communication, but they also need to inspect and analyze the supply lines. In some places in the world, the supply lines and infrastructure—such as water and power—can be unreliable and don't keep pace with urban growth. Even here in the US, some regions have experienced the pain associated with unreliable power and water. Gratefully, overall, the US has mostly reliable supply lines and infrastructure in place that have helped support growth. However, in places that struggle to keep up with demand, power access fluctuates and results in brownouts and blackouts. In some places, water pressure and cleanliness are limited and endangered by drought conditions or contamination. In places where infrastructure keeps pace with demand for water and power, growth can happen.

Countries that invest in infrastructure for the critical core elements of work and life, including power, water, and broadband internet access, for example, will have an advantage and opportunity to accelerate their economic growth in the future. It is imperative to keep them strong, reliable, and stable. Again, in some areas of the US, these vital pieces have seen some cracks in the system. We should heed early warnings and be proactive. The future depends on ensuring those systems remain strong. The country worked hard, over many decades, to build infrastructure and supply lines, but some aspects are now threatened by drought, high demand, wear, or other stressors. It is critical not to neglect attention to them so that we can continue to produce and grow.

As leaders look at the vital supply lines and infrastructure their organization requires, they need to consider the basic elements that will allow accelerated growth. If the revenue doubles or triples in a short time, ask whether space, power, water, and technology can support that kind of growth. The needs of every business are different, of course. Consider locations and how you will access these key elements. To what extent, for example, does transportation of people and goods impact your growth and expansion? What partners will you need to enlist? Accelerated growth and expansion will quickly harm an organization if you have not considered whether the supply lines are ready to support it.

Prepare Reinforcements

Finally, teach your new leaders to manage accelerated growth by preparing reinforcements. Every person has a finite, defined kind and amount of knowledge, stamina, experiences, and time. So, you must help leaders be aware of how and when to prepare reinforcements and identify additional talent to help share the workload. Leaders may show a high level of capacity and talent for work, so it is particularly important for you to model ways to invite other team members and equip and include them in the work. It is particularly critical when the organization is experiencing accelerated growth. There may be higher demand for the leader's time and additional or new tasks and steps, so it may feel very difficult to recruit, hire, and train additional support. But it is especially important at these times that leaders focus on securing that talent so that the acceleration is not inadvertently blunted due to insufficient workforce or the wrong talent and experience. It is better to slow the growth for a period to focus on getting the right team in place so that the organization has a strong trajectory of accelerated growth.

Help your leaders understand that during accelerated growth, they need to work on and in the business. Working on and in the business includes evaluating the infrastructure and personnel necessary for each phase of growth. For example, generally, one person can manage about eight to twelve associates effectively. When the team grows to between twelve and twenty, it is time to promote another manager to take on the team and determine how the workload will be shared across the teams. If you move too slowly, you risk burning out your people and managers.

Not only must you think about how to divide teams and add management to boost productivity, but also how to help leaders keep an eye out for the next senior-level leader who embraces the organization's growth and shows potential for steering it in the future.

LEAD EXPONENTIALLY

This work should never stop. As you might have realized by now, I hope that you are developing a leader who can develop other leaders! Without this focus and ability, your organization will never capitalize on accelerated growth times, and there is little likelihood you can build a sustainable, enduring organization. The key to accelerated growth is to prepare those reinforcements for what they will need to know and do, so that growth continues but you also stave off burnout. It is undoubtedly a tricky dance to do well. Leaders who want to build organizations must learn it.

Accelerated growth and expansion phases of an organization's history are so much fun to be a part of. For several consecutive years, our company has experienced expansion and revenue growth. We haven't always followed the preceding framework perfectly, but my personal purpose is through intuitive interaction, propelling leaders through their self-imposed barriers to live out their unique purpose in life. And accelerated growth in our firm has given me many chances to help build up and prepare our reinforcements, placing new leadership teams in place and helping fulfill our purpose as a company to bring peace of mind to more people and places. It's been a lot of fun!

As you identify and develop new leaders, be sure to include them in the adventure that is accelerated growth. Help them learn to monitor communications, inspect and analyze supply lines and infrastructure capacity, and, of course, prepare those reinforcements, so the team expands and grows at a rate commensurate with the needs of the current—and future—work. I hope you've had chances to experience this yourself! It is a peak experience for a leader to accelerate growth. It is highly rewarding and certainly intense, but effective leaders need to learn how to lead through it so that they can assume the roles required to keep the organization moving forward in the future.

CHAPTER 27

Future State

While I've noted and hinted at it in previous chapters, it is important to develop leaders to be consistently and continually future thinking, even as they respond to immediate and pressing needs. It is fun, as leaders, to lead organizations that are experiencing healthy, accelerated growth that meets or exceeds strategic plan goals. Growth is fun! The effect of growth spreads ripples that are sometimes not even possible to quantify as the organization's vision is accomplished and influence expands. When acceleration periods happen, and they are done in sustainable, thoughtful ways, leaders want it to keep going, of course. However, those phases inevitably end, as hyper growth really isn't sustainable forever. I've reflected on the changes in significant institutions, particularly the Christian church, whose growth has ebbed and flowed throughout its history. It's currently growing quickly in Africa and in Asia, specifically, but adherents to the faith are shrinking in Europe and North America, for example.

It feels uncertain when double-digit, year-over-year numbers begin to trend downward to single-digit growth or when stagnation occurs. Leaders need to have a forward-thinking mindset, anticipating what future trends look like, and then work to anticipate and prepare for that potential future state. It is maybe one of the most difficult things to develop new leaders around, since I think some naturally think about future things. Some people are naturally curious about things that happened in the past. Others tend to focus on the current state of things, and still others think mostly about what's next. All are valuable, but leaders responsible for the outcomes of the organization need to build their capacity to think about the future.

Help your future leaders learn to forecast, prepare, and beware of future possibilities. Many people speak dreamily about better tomorrows on the way. They tend to hope things will be better than they are today. It's not a bad way to think, for sure. Positive psychologists have described hopefulness as having a positive view of the future but also believing that you have the power to make that future happen.[1] The differentiator from just wishing for something better is the agency included in this model, namely, believing you have the power to make that future happen.

Many people are proactive about the future, generally believing it will get better, or even planning for a better future. Many people have a positive view of the future. As the *World Happiness Report* shows, many in high-poverty and war-torn areas of the world, understandably, have a gloomy view of the present, making it harder to envision a positive future state.[2]

It has been said that positive people are right some of the time, and they are happy with that outcome, while pessimists are right some of the time and are never happy with that outcome. It is so important to train leaders to understand, too, that their perspective on the future becomes a shared one. While leaders must be authentic and genuine, they must also work on crafting a positive view of the future that others can also share. It is a key part of leading well. However, how you think about the future may affect your disposition, and your disposition as a leader is always on display. So, leaders must learn to forecast and prepare for a most positive future. Teach your developing leaders that there must be a reasonable balance in their understanding of the potential future state. Leaders should maintain a level of positivity, but they likewise cannot be naive. Train your leaders to look for the good ahead and to view obstacles with eyes wide open. Refusing to acknowledge current or potential roadblocks does nothing to mitigate their impact. They will impede progress more than if they are not acknowledged.

I've said it before, but the power of the mind to envision a positive future state is important. Develop leaders who are inclined to commit to the creation of an enduring organization and help them learn to fix their mindset on that better future. Perspective is a starting point toward the next step of the journey of realizing that best future. Sharing that perspective with others to help the team remain motivated and focused will help your organization have the best chance of seeing better days ahead. Your leaders can begin the work of thinking about the future state by learning to forecast, prepare, and beware.

Forecast

When your mindset is fixed on the future, then it is time to forecast that future. It is amazing to me how often people look at the weather forecast. I don't spend as much time doing that personally, because I'm just fine only having a general idea of what the weather will be—hot, cold, windy, snowy, or rainy. Growing up and living in the Midwest means it's usually easy for me to adjust to whatever happens! I don't tend to complain much about the weather, and in most cases, it doesn't affect my day's purpose and work. I recognize that is not the case for many friends and neighbors, whose work is indeed impacted by the weather. The power workers are forever heroes, as tornadoes ravaged some parts of our city recently, and it will take a long time for those families to recover. But we were all grateful for the quick work of the power teams, who restored power for those whose homes were not otherwise affected by the storm. I've noticed, in my travels, that even in places where the weather tends to have less variance than ours does in the Midwest, like the West Coast or Hawaii, people are still very attentive to the weather forecast.

Unlike the weather forecast, though, which generally extends to the next week or so, forecasting conditions internally and externally to your organization must be long term. Some climatologists and meteorologists certainly have a long view regarding weather pattern changes over time, but most of us are not so familiar with the research! So, we resort to viewing and digesting the information we know for our immediate future. In your organization, forecasting should occur for the next week, certainly, but must include analysis of past and current data to create scenarios and plans for the next month, quarter, year, and even into the next decade or more. To do this, leaders should identify the right metrics and data to observe past and predict potential future trends so that the plans can be generated accordingly.

I encourage leaders to look at traditional past and current financial metrics, for example, (i.e., the previous year's quarter is the starting point for forecasting the next five years for that same quarter), but they must also look at the qualitative data, which is sometimes more difficult to quantify as they forecast. For example, what do we understand and know about what challenges teams faced during the highest growth times and how does it inform our forecast for how we meet the team's needs for the next anticipated high growth time? It might go without saying that our predictions cannot always be correct, any more than the meteorologists get it right all the time. However, being in the proverbial ballpark is usually what is needed to make informed decisions. Teach your leaders that, over time, they can—with strong review and reflection—refine their forecasting by analyzing what they got right and what they did not.

Help your leaders identify factors that are unchanging. This might be your headquarters or store location, the business lines, or the kind of talent you hire. Then consider what it is that ought to change. Our company determined we needed a rebrand and logo update a couple of years ago (see Signal Timeline in Chapter 19, page 147). It was uncomfortable for everyone but needed. We knew by looking ahead that our current brand was not going to support the growth we wanted to see globally, so we tackled the planning and got it done. It was the right change and has been received well in the market.

Prepare

I've been able to forecast the growth opportunity for our business within the industrial segment near our headquarters. With that anticipated growth, we move to preparing for it—the next step. Teach leaders that when preparing for the future state, you look at what you have and what you need to be successful.

Outside of Omaha, Nebraska, where our company is based, there is going to be a huge construction project to build infrastructure for distribution and transportation of goods. This area has rail running through it, and the land is reasonably priced and accessible. Knowing this is being planned helps other nearby businesses anticipate the arrival of new jobs to the area, and it may result in elevating property values surrounding the build. For our business, our corporate location is not going to change in the future, nor will our other areas of service. However, what will change is the addition of other development and businesses in the region, which might result in a need for our services in that specific area. Knowing this has informed some of our business decisions for our area franchises.

Sometimes it can make leaders feel overwhelmed as they consider the future, look at what they have, and realize they're grossly underprepared. Always begin the assessment of what you have with the end in mind. In other words, it's OK that you aren't yet prepared. The fact that you're looking toward the future is what helps you know that you need to adjust and adapt to that future state, which isn't here yet. Thank goodness!

Let your leaders know they don't have to be the only one who works toward clarity about what is needed. Rely on the process outlined earlier of asking good questions of the right people. Many are available to help leaders get clear about what is needed to plan. You can let your leaders know that they need to look at people, products, and processes.

People, Products, and Processes

Encourage your leaders to first look for the talent they need to support the future work of the organization. Think about talents, skills, and expertise. These are not all the same. Consider what things are strong and what elements are missing from the team. There are many resources to lean on now to help onboard that talent to get them ready, but the leader should first think about relationships and ensuring that there is a clear plan for connecting new talent with existing talent in the organization.

Next, have your leaders consider the products—the stuff—that will be required to ensure the organization can succeed. This varies by sector, and may even be specific to the organization, but could include supplies, furniture, inventory, buildings/space, software and technology, and so many other things. If your leader has a strong detail orientation, this might be easier for them to understand, but if the leader you're developing is not so detail oriented, be sure to steer them to get support in considering this piece. Steer toward analyzing the current product needs and use that to help project and forecast what will be required for the future state of the organization.

When you've got the people and product list assembled, the future starts to seem a bit clearer. But leaders also need to consider additional or new processes to be ready for the future. Consider whether current processes are the right ones for the future work. Think about the people and what they will be doing and how their expertise and work will change workflow, communications, document management, HR, etc.

The intent is for you to give leaders a helpful framework to understand what things they need to think about or know to help steer the organization toward the future. Remember that teams and people may require different things for work, and account for those differences.

Beware

In preparing for the future state of the organization, your leaders should forecast, prepare, and, finally, beware. It is a critical piece of the leadership puzzle to solve. It's important that developing leaders learn not to get too far ahead of themselves. Establish concrete milestones and commitments, and reforecast, if needed, when things need to be adjusted. Leaders will need to plan for the unexpected, since there is no way to predict everything that will happen. The global COVID pandemic was a tough teacher for everyone, from 2020 to 2021. Few organizations could plan for such a disastrous event. While it is critical to teach leaders to have contingencies, there are times when the utterly improbable shows up to change it all. Nonetheless, contingency thinking is an asset that leaders need to learn and be prepared to employ—for big and small things.

A couple of years ago, our company planned an outside event at a hotel in Miami, in January. I picked this location in January specifically due to the temperate weather that time of year. Lo and behold, the day before our event, there was a forecast for severe storms and maybe even a tornado. It was unusual and unexpected. However, the hotel had a contingency plan and moved the event indoors. The show went on. This was just a single event, and the contingency plan was important, since many attendees were impacted. It is even more critical to have organization-wide contingencies based on what happens with your organization in the future. To beware of the future is thoughtful, not pessimistic. While it is critical for you to teach leaders the importance of a positive vision and mindset for the future, contingency thinking is thorough thinking. It is necessary to ensure continued progress, as well as quick recovery, should the most difficult scenarios materialize.

As you develop leaders, you must encourage them to practice pondering what the future state of the organization looks like. You will encourage them to have a positive mindset with a clear vision of the best possible future. Teach them the tools of forecasting the future—considering people, products, and processes—so they can then prepare accordingly. Then, help them own the responsibility for the future by teaching them to beware of the possible scenarios and to be ready with contingencies that the organization can fall back on if crazy things happen, as they reliably do. Once you've grounded them in future thinking, it's, finally, time to boost their ability to triplicate.

CHAPTER 28

Triplicate

You now have a foundation for understanding why you should identify and develop leaders. You've considered who you should look to invest in, what things they should know, and where in the organization they could use their leadership skills. Finally, we've discussed more about how to develop those leaders, and you've reviewed how to help leaders endure and create sustainable, strong practices.

As you invest in your leader, you're giving them the tools they need to lead, and a by-product of effective leadership is enduring, purposeful organizations that stand the test of time—organizations whose vision and purpose strengthen people and communities. The principles and frameworks here are designed not only to help scale effective leadership for today but to ensure continual effective leadership in the future. If that doesn't happen, there will be no enduring organization. History reflects that it is rare to create an enduring organization. Most organizations don't stand the test of time. In fact, the average lifespan of organizations is currently about twenty years and appears to be shrinking.[1] I'm not comfortable with that trend! I want to build an organization with a vision and purpose that is carried forward and creates opportunities for many people to live good lives and to have peace of mind for decades to come. I want the organization to endure beyond my tenure and leadership to the next generation and the one after that. I am inspired by the few businesses left in the US that have been around about as long as the nation has, such as the King Arthur Baking Company, formerly King Arthur Flour, founded in 1790. Their history as the oldest flour company in the United States is storied. Their flour has been in use since Martha Washington baked her apple pies![2] The *New York Post* is one of the oldest published papers, founded in 1801,[3] and Jim Beam has been distilling whiskey since 1795.[4] Strong, effective leaders propel a purpose and a vision forward for others to benefit. Start by sharing the vision and purpose for leadership with your protégés, then continue to share the principles, frameworks, and tools they need to be successful.

Replicate Is OK; Triplicate Is Better

I'd suggest that you can increase the probability of success of developing effective leaders who support and sustain your organization over the long term by triplicating your effort. You did read that correctly! I want you to triplicate your effort, not just duplicate it. If you identify and develop one potential leader, you, of course, duplicate your knowledge and experience. There is one individual at a time you focus upon. This method has its advantages: You're able to listen well to one voice and respond to their needs. You can be more assured of what they need and remain attentive to their next steps as you place them in the leadership role. Of course, no one takes what they have learned and perfectly mirrors those learnings. Things change, people change, and, of course, leaders you identify and invest in will take the wheel and, hopefully, lead others in their own way. They may also opt to exit the organization and bring their learnings elsewhere. Sometimes that is tough, but it can be rewarding when a strong leader shows their value in another space.

To *replicate* leadership knowledge and skills sounds a bit more systematic or even programmatic. Of course, this book isn't so much about a program as it is about sharing experiences and frameworks to help leaders fill gaps in knowledge and thinking, so they have support as they lead. A system or program that replicates the leadership-development process sounds good—and could even be helpful—as it has high levels of scalability and potential success, at least in the short term. When teachers and learners are looking to replicate leadership lessons and learnings via a program, it can be like a well-oiled machine, and keeps that engine running. However, undoubtedly, the system and program will need to be changed and updated continually over time, if the principles and lessons become outdated. Someone will need to innovate and reposition the system as the world or the organization's circumstances shift.

So, I offer a slightly different perspective or principle for multiplying your leadership for your protégés. You should *triplicate*—the verb form of creating three of something. In practice, it's simple, but I think this principle could make a big difference in the long term. To start, as you select a leader to develop, identify one who is already investing in and developing another leader—someone who seems to already be a leader of leaders. Theoretically, you have multiple leaders in queue with this model, and you are assured of finding someone who is already influencing others and, presumably, the organization. In this model, you are developing a leader. Your learner is also developing a leader. So, there are three individuals influenced by this leadership-development pipeline. I'm not concerned with whether the leader you develop has just one person reporting to them or if they are more informally mentoring someone else. The model is designed to help expand vision for the purpose of the organization over time and through varying perspectives.

I enjoy studying the Bible and biblical times and applying those lessons learned in life, leadership, and learning. Christians have a Trinitarian view of God as Father, Son, and Holy Spirit. This so-called three-in-one understanding of God has a completeness about it that is reassuring, as it informs how God has made Himself known and how we can relate with Him. I believe that the perfect, relational completeness of the Triune God is inspiring for the ways we can serve and lead others.

In a triplicate model of leadership development, there is an established leader, a practicing leader, and an emerging leader in a developmental triad. Each leader is learning and imparting knowledge and sharing experiences that do not happen when a more linear view of leadership development is implemented via systems, programs, or even one-one-one mentorship. This model is valuable in identifying and developing leaders because it helps reduce the effect of bias by opening eyes to see things from another's view and expands the information and data needed to fulfill the work and tasks of leadership.

Triplicate:
A Model for Leadership Development

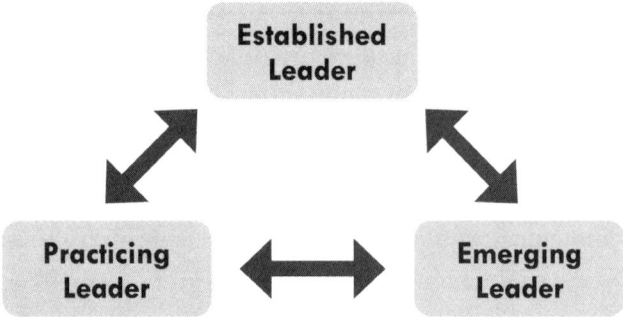

Established Leaders

I have presumed a bit that since you are reading this book, you are an established leader who is eager to identify and develop other leaders. I suggest that you, as an established leader, must safeguard and communicate the purpose—the why—of the organization. You must drive the purpose forward. For established leaders, who have some tenure in the organization, you likely have the best view of past successes, present state, and future possibilities. Strategically, you've seen ideas come and go: some that worked and some that did not. That is invaluable experience to share as you develop practicing leaders. You can name and identify current, practicing leaders who have potential for developing as leaders themselves, and who also have begun to invest in others. You can encourage your leaders to embrace the idea of accelerated, exponential growth and that they do so with a focus on benefiting others, owning the responsibility of providing for the needs of today *and* for tomorrow. You know the stories about how the organization arrived at where it is. Those are valuable lore and data that can inspire and inform practicing and emerging leaders.

I've shared my love for history. I've reflected a lot on the Depression era, which my grandparents lived through. I often felt confounded by their propensity to be extremely frugal, even miserly. I noticed that my grandparents and others of their peer group did not generously tip for service, for example. And they, in fact, rarely ate out, and if they did, it was at the least expensive dining establishments. They often wore clothes until they were threadbare and had far fewer options in their wardrobe. When my grandparents bought their first house and car, they intended to keep them indefinitely. Unless something significant changed, like adding a family member or the car stopped running altogether, they didn't buy a different one. They kept their things until they simply didn't run or work any longer. They didn't buy a different one simply because their tastes changed. They didn't have the consumptive habits that we maintain today. They also tended to stay at the same job or same company for many years, and kept canned, well-preserved food in the pantry.

I deeply regret my, along with my siblings and peers, lack of understanding and childish mocking of some of these behaviors. One day, I thought to ask, "Why?" I learned that the Great Depression drove these habits that became engrained. They adopted a scarcity mindset for the sake of survival because everything that everyone needed was, indeed, terrifyingly scarce. Many starved, and those who did survive vowed to protect themselves and those they loved by protecting and guarding resources for the worst possible contingency, which they had experienced. My frame of reference was changed, and I had such respect for their struggles and their story. I aimed to resist extreme consumption, which is so commonplace and easy to indulge with our easy access to online and brick-and-mortar retail stores. I learned that you cannot sit and wait, but rather you must go and do. Their generation's focus on character and remaining true to your word is a key part of effective and successful leadership, which I saw modeled. And I also appreciate that today, for some, there is more autonomy to select the kind of work and life you wish to build.

An established leader will also have a strong understanding of the "who" of your organization—who to identify as a leader. I am influenced by the lives and the values present among members of the so-called Greatest Generation. There's certainly a reason Tom Brokaw called them that in his book by the same name.[5] I think that they understood that their character was important. They valued it greatly, and I fear that some of their ideals are harder to find in practice today. It is critical that, as an established leader, you find those of high character to invest in so that their ideals can be shared and shown to others. The past is an important teacher. As an established leader, use the lessons of the past to inform your development of that next-generation, practicing leader. You can teach them why the organization chooses to operate the way it does and provide perspective that can inform their decisions for the future.

Practicing Leaders

A practicing leader likely has strong insights about the "what" and the "where" for your organization—what to do and where to make it happen—as they're firmly entrenched in the organization's happenings at this stage of their career. They understand processes and who is working on them and can bring strong awareness of the present state and relevant data to different levels of the organization. They can serve as a sort of relational and communication hub to build awareness and understanding between established and emerging leaders. As practicing leaders with some experience and involvement in core areas of the organization, they can share what others need to know and do and where knowledge and skills need to change, grow, and be applied in the organization. An easier time and place to analyze for the organization is invariably the present time and place, but it is still easy to miss key indicators. It is important that assessment and analysis each continue as leaders work through their weeks and quarters.

Emerging Leaders

An emerging leader, new and ready to learn, might have the strong ability to inform the "how"—how to move the organization forward. They will focus on the future state, bring new ideas, and have the most amount of time to help create it. They will initiate new frameworks that you will help them implement and adjust based on internal and environmental changes. Emerging leaders will learn and apply what their predecessors share with them, ideally, leveraging what is timeless but innovating what is needed to be sustainable.

The emerging leaders, again, must be taught to look forward—to imagine and to dream. They must resist inertia and be ready to initiate new things. When emerging leaders begin to take on new roles, sometimes existing processes, systems, and expectations seem so embedded that it can be difficult to take initiative and innovate. But with the consistently changing world, it is imperative that they practice and that established leaders provide the space and room to try and fail and then try once again.

I am inspired by the life and ministry of the young pastor Timothy in the Bible. With the Apostle Paul as his mentor, he began to lead and had the encouragement and development he needed to do so effectively. He and other early, young apprentices of Jesus helped set the Christian faith on a path to expansion. I'm grateful for the legacy of faithfulness and leaders who developed other leaders so that the faith endured.

To create an enduring organization that stands the test of time, consider leadership development in triplicate: develop a leader who is also leading someone else. Create a community of three leaders—an established leader, a practicing leader, and an emerging leader—to have a lens of the who, what, when, where, why, and how to help inform the past, present, and future state of your organization. Whether you are an established, practicing, or emerging leader, if you are curious about additional ideas to help others learn and fulfill their purpose each moment, day, and week, you might find my first book, *Transform through Purpose*, helpful in this regard. You will need to ensure that your leaders do not work in a default mode, but are intentional, putting principles, plans, processes, and systems in place.

Above all, as you develop leaders, keep your focus on your protégé rather than yourself. Selfishness is the death knell of many an organization. Center the purpose and keep people in the middle, so your organization does not fade or fail. When you're developing leaders, look to the past and work intentionally in the present while maintaining a mindset on the future. Rely on your team of leaders in a developmental mindset that is humble and always growing, having the benefit of every group in mind. I always say that the more our company grows, the more people I am working for—not the other way around.

It is my hope that you want to make a difference with your organization for generations to come. Triplicate your leadership. Embrace and share the principles and frameworks in this book. Developing leaders is such a challenging ask, but it is incredibly rewarding. It is a lifelong commitment. Thank you for your commitment, your sacrifice, and your investment. Begin today to lead exponentially. Your efforts will result in transforming individuals, and the ripples are endless, as strong leaders develop other strong leaders, and the purpose lives on.

Notes

Preface

1. "Average Company Lifespan on Standard and Poor's 500 Index from 1965 to 2030, in Years," Statista, https://www.statista.com/statistics/1259275/average-company-lifespan/.

2. Jena McGregor, "Why America's Founding Fathers Wanted the President to Take a Salary," *The Washington Post*, March 15, 2017, https://www.washingtonpost.com/news/on-leadership/wp/2017/03/15/why-americas-founding-fathers-wanted-the-president-to-take-a-salary/.

Chapter 1

1. Amy Adkins, "Only One in 10 People Possess the Talent to Manage," Gallup, April 13, 2015, https://www.gallup.com/workplace/236579/one-people-possess-talent-manage.aspx.

2. Alison Dachner and Erin Makarius, "Turn Departing Employees into Loyal Alumni," *Harvard Business Review*, March–April 2021, https://hbr.org/2021/03/turn-departing-employees-into-loyal-alumni.

Chapter 2

1. "Culture Eats Strategy for Breakfast," DailyAgile, https://dailyagile.com/culture-eats-strategy-for-breakfast/.

2. Jim Clifton and Jim Harter, *It's the Manager* (Washington, DC: Gallup Press, 2019), 131–133.

Chapter 3

1. Mark Maloy, "'First in Peace' George Washington During 1783–1789," American Battlefield Trust, May 1, 2020, https://www.battlefields.org/learn/articles/first-peace-george-washington-during-1783-1789.
2. Stephen Juza, "2023 NFL Head Coach Trees," Pro-Football-History.com, https://pro-football-history.com/blog/10/46/2023-nfl-head-coach-trees.
3. Matthew 4:18.
4. John Mark Comer, *Practicing the Way: Be with Jesus. Become like Him. Do as He Did*, (Colorado Springs, CO: WaterBrook, 2024).
5. Happiness Council, *Global Happiness and Well-Being Policy Report*, 2019, https://www.happinesscouncil.org/report/2019/global-happiness-and-well-being-policy-report.

Chapter 4

1. "DeWalt vs. Black & Decker: Which of the Two Brands Is Better?" Handyman's World, March 4, 2020, https://handymansworld.net/dewalt-vs-black-decker/.

Chapter 5

1. Philippians 2:5.
2. Lydia Saad, "Stable US Moral Ratings Obscure Big Partisan Shifts," Gallup, June 16, 2021, https://news.gallup.com/poll/351140/stable-moral-ratings-obscure-big-partisan-shifts.aspx?utm_source=alert&utm_medium=email&utm_content=morelink&utm_campaign=syndication.
3. John 13:1–17.

Notes

Chapter 6

1. Ronald Riggio, "What Is Charisma and Charismatic Leadership?" *Psychology Today*, October 7, 2012, https://www.psychologytoday.com/us/blog/cutting-edge-leadership/201210/what-is-charisma-and-charismatic-leadership.

Chapter 7

1. "Median Years of Tenure with Current Employer for Employed Wage and Salary Workers in the United States from 2010 to 2022," Statista, https://www.statista.com/statistics/1174504/us-employed-workers-median-years-tenure/.
2. Jason Fuller, "Welcome to the Portal—Where College Athletes Can Risk It All for a Shot at Glory," NPR, May 19, 2023, https://www.npr.org/2023/05/19/1173134544/college-football-transfer-portal-ncaa-student-athlete.
3. *Encyclopaedia Britannica Online*, s.v. "Ernest Shackleton," September 20, 2024, https://www.britannica.com/biography/Ernest-Henry-Shackleton.
4. "Marie Curie: Facts about the Pioneering Chemist," History.com, February 22, 2021, https://www.history.com/news/marie-curie-facts.

Chapter 8

1. David Vergun, "Modernization of Armed Forces a Collaborative Effort, Official Says," US Department of Defense, September 12, 2022, https://www.defense.gov/News/News-Stories/Article/Article/3155206/modernization-of-armed-forces-a-collaborative-effort-official-says/.

Chapter 12

1. Matthew 5:42.
2. Luke 15.

3. Mark 12:42.
4. Matthew 6:19.
5. Luke 20:46–47.

Chapter 13

1. "Panama Canal," History.com, August 13, 2024, https://www.history.com/topics/landmarks/panama-canal.
2. *Encyclopaedia Britannica Online*, s.v. "American Intervention in Panama Canal," October 23, 2024, https://www.britannica.com/topic/Panama-Canal/American-intervention.

Chapter 14

1. Richard Feloni, "Former Navy Seal Officer Explains the Most Valuable Leadership Lesson SEALs Learn in Hell Week," *Business Insider*, October 28, 2015, https://www.businessinsider.com/former-seal-officer-shares-the-top-lesson-from-buds-training-2015-10.

Chapter 15

1. Jim Harter, "Disengagement Persists Among US Employees," Gallup, April 25, 2022, https://www.gallup.com/workplace/391922/employee-engagement-slump-continues.aspx.
2. Adelle Waldman, "It's Not Just Wages. Retailers Are Mistreating Workers in a More Insidious Way," *The New York Times*, February 19, 2024, https://www.nytimes.com/2024/02/19/opinion/part-time-workers-usa.html.
3. "Civilian Unemployment Rate," US Bureau of Labor Statistics, accessed September 27, 2024, https://www.bls.gov/charts/employment-situation/civilian-unemployment-rate.htm.
4. Robert Fulghum, *All I Really Need to Know I Learned in Kindergarten: Uncommon Thoughts on Common Things* (New York: Ivy Books, 1988).

Notes

5. Jack Zenger and Joseph Folkman, "Quiet Quitting Is About Bad Bosses, Not Bad Employees," *Harvard Business Review*, August 31, 2022, https://hbr.org/2022/08/quiet-quitting-is-about-bad-bosses-not-bad-employees.

6. Jim Harter, "US Employee Engagement Needs a Rebound in 2023," Gallup, January 25, 2023, https://www.gallup.com/workplace/468233/employee-engagement-needs-rebound-2023.aspx.

Chapter 16

1. Randall Beck and Jim Harter, "Managers Account for 70% of Variance in Employee Engagement," Gallup, April 21, 2015, https://news.gallup.com/businessjournal/182792/managers-account-variance-employee-engagement.aspx.

2. Ryan Pendell, "Employee Engagement Strategies: Fixing the World's $8.8 Trillion Problem," Gallup, June 14, 2022, https://www.gallup.com/workplace/393497/world-trillion-workplace-problem.aspx.

3. Beck and Harter, "Managers Account for 70%."

4. Justin Bariso, "Gallup Research Says This 15-Minute Weekly Habit Boosts Employee Engagement and Strengthens Relationships," MSN, January 24, 2024, https://www.msn.com/en-us/money/smallbusiness/gallup-research-says-this-15-minute-weekly-habit-boosts-employee-engagement-and-strengthens-relationships/ar-BB1hfQFJ?ocid=entnewsntp&pc=DCTS&cvid=3b4b76fd37214b1ab9016f9956ef4d98&ei=17.

5. Clifton and Harter, *It's the Manager*, 75–120.

6. Andrew Syrios, "Performance Bonuses Don't Motivate People. Here's What Does," AlleyWatch, January 2019, https://www.alleywatch.com/2019/01/performance-bonuses-dont-motivate-people-heres-what-does/.

Chapter 18

1. Frederic Funck, "Executives Are Denying Their Stress and That's a Problem—Here's How to Cope," *Forbes*, April 13, 2021, https://www.forbes.com/sites/forbescoachescouncil/2021/04/13/executives-are-denying

-their-stress-and-thats-a-problem---heres-how-to-cope/; Jeffrey Pfeffer, *Dying for a Paycheck: How Modern Management Harms Employee Health and Company Performance and What We Can Do about It* (Harper Business: 2018).

2. Tomas Chamorro-Premuzic, "5 Ways Leaders Accidentally Stress Out Their Employees," *Harvard Business Review*, May 11, 2020, https://hbr.org/2020/05/5-ways-leaders-accidentally-stress-out-their-employees.

3. Matthew 26:69–74.

4. John 21:15–19.

5. Shaan Madhavji, "Leadership Bias: How to Identify and Overcome It," EHL Insights, September 27, 2023, https://hospitalityinsights.ehl.edu/leadership-bias.

6. Christian Stadler, "What Is the Secret to Walmart's Success?" *Forbes*, May 24, 2024, https://www.forbes.com/sites/christianstadler/2024/05/24/what-is-the-secret-to-walmarts-success/.

7. David Trainer, "Target's Innovation Continues to Drive Value," *Forbes*, September 18, 2019, https://www.forbes.com/sites/greatspeculations/2019/09/18/targets-innovation-continues-to-drive-value/.

8. David Porter, "Kmart Was Once a Retail Powerhouse. Now Just a Handful of Stores Remain in the US," PBS, April 11, 2022, https://www.pbs.org/newshour/nation/kmart-was-once-a-retail-powerhouse-now-just-a-handful-of-stores-remain-in-the-u-s.

Chapter 19

1. Aaron Goldburg, *Buying Disney's World: The Story of How Florida's Swampland Became Walt Disney World* (Quaker Scribe Publishing, 2021): 3–6.

2. Ben Popken and Tom Costello, "Tens of Thousands of Airline Workers Are Out of Jobs After Congress Fails to Reach Deal," NBC News, September 30, 2020, https://www.nbcnews.com/business/economy/around-35-000-people-could-lose-their-job-tonight-if-n1241588.

3. "George Washington Unanimously Elected First US President," History, This Day in History, https://www.history.com/this-day-in-history/first-u-s-president-elected.

Chapter 21

1. Tom Rath and Barry Conchie, *Strengths Based Leadership* (Washington, DC: Gallup Press, 2008): 21.
2. Tom Osborne and John E. Roberts, *More than Winning: The Story of Tom Osborne* (Lincoln, NE: University of Nebraska Press, 1985).

Chapter 22

1. "Impact Overview," TOMS, https://www.toms.com/en-us/impact/.

Chapter 24

1. Greg Niemann, *Big Brown: The Untold Story of UPS* (Hoboken, NJ: John Wiley & Sons, Inc., 2007).
2. *Encyclopaedia Britannica Online*, s.v. "New Coke," September 25, 2024, https://www.britannica.com/topic/New-Coke.
3. Jordan Valinsky, "McDonald's Is Returning the Egg McMuffin to its Original Price," CNN, November 17, 2021, https://www.cnn.com/2021/11/16/business/mcdonalds-egg-mcmuffin-deal/index.html.
4. Becky Little, "Who Invented Buffalo Wings?" History, May 5, 2023, https://www.history.com/news/who-invented-buffalo-wings.
5. Liliana M. Esposito, "The History of Wendy's Chili Recipe," Wendy's, February 22, 2018, https://www.wendys.com/blog/chili-recipe-isnt-your-family-recipe-but-its-pretty-darn-close.

Chapter 25

1. Brian Brim, "Strengths-Based Leadership: The 4 Things Followers Need," Gallup, October 9, 2015, https://www.gallup.com/cliftonstrengths/en/251003/strengths-based-leadership-things-followers-need.aspx.

Chapter 26

1. Malcolm Gladwell, "How to Start an Epidemic," *The Guardian*, April 22, 2000, https://www.theguardian.com/books/2000/apr/22/extract.

Chapter 27

1. Shane Lopez, *Making Hope Happen: Create the Future You Want for Yourself and Others* (New York: Atria, 2014): 18.
2. World Happiness Report, *World Happiness Report 2024*, https://worldhappiness.report/.

Chapter 28

1. D. Clark, "Average Company Lifespan on Standard and Poor's 500 Index from 1965 to 2030, in Years," Statista, August 12, 2024, https://www.statista.com/statistics/1259275/average-company-lifespan/.
2. "Our History," King Arthur Baking, https://www.kingarthurbaking.com/history.
3. New York Post, "About New York Post," 2025, https://nypost.com/about-new-york-post/#.
4. "Jim Beam Founders," Whiskey University, accessed January 29, 2025, https://www.whiskeyuniv.com/jim-beam-founders.
5. Tom Brokaw, *The Greatest Generation* (New York: Random House, 1998).

About the Author

Photo by Elise Nyffeler

Reed Nyffeler is a lifelong entrepreneur with a passion for developing the next generation of leaders, finding solutions, and implementing growth strategies. As the CEO and founder of Signal, he has led the fast-growing, industry-leading security services franchisor with a mission to provide peace of mind to pursue passion in life. He is also the author of *Transform through Purpose: Your Path to Living an Authentic and Intentional Life*.

Through intentionality grounded in an unshakeable faith, Nyffeler has learned to identify his priorities and to passionately pursue his purpose in every area of his life. He carefully balances his professional aspirations with time spent enjoying and connecting with his happy, thriving family of six.